ON THE
STATE
OF EGYPT

ALAA AL ASWANY

ON THE
STATE
OF EGYPT

A NOVELIST'S PROVOCATIVE REFLECTIONS

TRANSLATED BY
JONATHAN WRIGHT

THE AMERICAN UNIVERSITY IN CAIRO PRESS
CAIRO NEW YORK

First published in 2011 by
The American University in Cairo Press
113 Sharia Kasr el Aini, Cairo, Egypt
420 Fifth Avenue, New York, NY 10018
www.aucpress.com

Dar el Kutub No. 19782/10
ISBN 978 977 416 461 3

Dar el Kutub Cataloging-in-Publication Data

Al Aswany, Alaa
        On the State of Egypt: A Novelist's Provocative Reflections / Alaa Al Aswany.— Cairo:
    The American University in Cairo Press, 2011
            p.   cm.
        ISBN 978 977 416 461 3
        1. Democracy-Egypt I. Title
        323.0420962

1 2 3 4 5 6   14 13 12 11

Designed by Fatiha Bouzidi
Printed in Egypt

Contents

Introduction   vii

The Presidency and Succession   1

The Egyptian Campaign against the Succession   3

Three Fallacious Arguments for Supporting Gamal Mubarak   7

The Art of Pleasing the President   11

The Chameleons Attack ElBaradei   15

Should Gaza Pay the Price for Hereditary Succession in Egypt?   19

Why Are We Falling Behind as the World Progresses?   23

The Only Way to Evict Mr. Battista   27

What Do Egyptians Expect from ElBaradei?   31

When Will President Mubarak Grasp This Truth?   35

Does Rigging Elections Count as a Major Sin?   39

Do We Need a Benevolent Dictator?   43

A Story for Children and Adults   47

A Surprise Dinner with an Important Person   51

Thoughts on the President's Health   57

Why Don't Egyptians Take Part in Elections?   61

The People and Social Justice   65

Our Advice to the Butcher   67

The Party of the Great Collapse   73

Why Do Egyptians Harass Women?   79

How Should We Overcome the Temptation Posed by Women? 83

The *Niqab* and Flawed Religiosity 87

Piety in Front of the Camera 91

What Will Protect the Copts? 95

Egypt Sits on the Substitutes' Bench 99

Are Egyptians Really Religious? 103

The Sorrows of Miss Laurence 107

Why Are Religious Fanatics Obsessed with Women's Bodies? 111

Nora and the National Squad 115

Defending Egypt's Flag 119

The Importance of Being Human 123

Who Killed the Egyptians on the Religious Holiday? 127

Can President Obama Save the Copts? 131

Egypt Awakened 135

The Story of Mamdouh Hamza 139

Who Is Killing the Poor in Egypt? 143

Does Subservience Protect Us from Injustice? 147

Does Mistreating People Invalidate the Ramadan Fast? 151

Free Speech and State Repression **155**

How Do Police Officers Celebrate Ramadan? 157

A Discussion with a State Security Officer 161

Four Videos to Entertain President Mubarak 165

Before We Damn Switzerland 169

An Unfortunate Incident Befalls a State Security Officer 173

Why Was the General Screaming? 177

Should We Start with Moral Reform or Reforming the System? 181

Are Freedoms Inseparable? 185

The Fate of Ibrahim Eissa 189

Introduction

I n 2004 I took part in a literary seminar held in New York City and, when the floor was opened to questions, a young American raised his hand, jumped up, and asked me the following question: "Do you Arabs have sex with women in the same way as us westerners?" The audience murmured and tittered for a while. In response I said, "As far as I know, people make love the same way all over the world, but one must always try to improve one's performance." The whole room burst out laughing and most of the audience thought it was a joke that relieved the seriousness of the discussion. When the seminar was over, the young man came up to me and asked politely if his question had annoyed me. I said no and shook his hand warmly. Then he said, "In fact I saw in a television program that in some ancient civilizations when men have sex they completely cover the woman's body with a sheet, leaving just a small opening."

I looked at the young man's face and he seemed wholly innocent. He really did not know what these Arabs do with their women and he expected them to do all kinds of strange and exceptional things, as we might expect from creatures coming from outer space. This incident illustrates the vast and ever-growing gap between the West and the Arab world. Westerners' knowledge of Arabs and Muslims was meager and superficial in the first place. What happened in the Islamic world was never a priority for the western media and the news was usually framed to suit the interests of western powers. So a despotic Arab ruler, for example, whatever crimes he committed against his own people, was called moderate and wise as long as he served the interests of the West. But if he rebelled against those inter-ests, he immediately became a dictator and all his crimes were exposed and publicized. Resisting U.S. occupation was always seen as terrorism, while resisting Soviet occupation was heroic and glorious. Then came the terrorist attacks of 9/11, which were a major turning point and confirmed to many westerners their image of Arabs as beings different from white westerners. They were seen as less inclined to work, as lazy and lascivious, as people who treat women as sex objects, and, most dangerous of all, as people who by nature and by culture are prone to violence and killing.

The anti-Arab and anti-Muslim articles the western press now publishes without any scruples would have been considered unacceptably reactionary and racist two decades ago, but unfortunately the floodgates of hatred have been opened wide. On dozens of western television programs people described as experts on the Middle East appear as guests to discuss why Islam is a violent religion that advocates killing people. Many of these experts are pitifully and disgracefully ignorant about Islamic culture and many of them follow whatever is the prevalent mood. If the western mind is inclined to blame all Muslims for terrorist crimes, then the experts always have to speak along those lines. None of them will ever mention that Arab and Muslim victims of terrorism far outnumber western victims, or the fact that Islam, like all religions, can be read either in a humane and magnanimous way or, erroneously, in a way that incites people to commit crimes. No one will ever mention that religion, any religion, cannot be responsible for those who misunderstand it. No one will point out that, when it was misread, the Christian religion, which taught mankind love and tolerance, led to the Crusades and the Inquisition, in which tens of thousands of innocent people were killed. But that does not give us the right to believe that Christianity incites to violence. None of them will mention all of this or take it into consideration. The more clearcut the prevalent stereotype, the more reassuring it is. Every Arab is in fact a potential terrorist, however educated or cultured he or she may be.

Over the last few years I have traveled to western countries dozens of times to promote my books and meet my readers. At airports I am not a renowned author, just an Arab passenger, a potential terrorist, and a free and easy target for anyone who feels like putting his or her hatred of Arabs and Muslims into practice. I'm not objecting to the security measures, I'm talking about an offensive hostility that has nothing to do with security: those searching looks of hatred and contempt some security officers give you just because you have Arab features or because your wife is wearing the *hijab*. You will be completely humiliated and then realize that you have no grounds for complaint. These officers are trained to deliver their humiliations gently. They slap you viciously in the face but they wear kid gloves that do not leave a mark. I will never forget the Egyptian girl in *hijab* when a security woman at Charles de Gaulle Airport forced her to take off her coat, although she was wearing nothing else but her underwear. I will never forget her face, crying in fright and humiliation, as she went through the electronic scanner in her underwear in full view of all the passengers.

Once, at Nice airport, after I had completed all the procedures like other passengers and I was only a few steps from the street, a French officer appeared, licking his lips like a cat stalking a mouse in a cartoon. He beckoned me with one finger as if to show how insignificant I was. He examined my passport, gave me a searching look full of hatred and contempt, and then asked, "What are you doing in France?"

I was surprised and did not answer. He repeated his question more loudly, "Do you understand French? What are you doing here?"

"I've come to France to look for good cows," I told him.

"Cows?" he asked with surprise, which showed me he was not gifted with great intelligence.

"Yes, I want to buy cows in France," I answered calmly and with a completely serious expression.

"But in your passport it says you're a dentist," he said.

"Now you know that some dentists like cows," I replied.

Only then did my message get through, and the man looked furious. We stood staring at each other for a full thirty seconds. I was determined not to look away, even if it meant spending the night in jail. At last the officer backed off, gave me my passport, and let me go out to the street. I should mention that I enjoy a large measure of immunity: I am a well-known writer, I speak French, I have a three-year visa to visit Europe, and I had been invited to lecture on Arabic literature at the Institute for Political Studies in Menton. If I, despite all that, was treated in this way, you can easily imagine what this officer might do to a woman in *hijab* who does not speak French or to a simple Arab man.

A wave of hatred for Arabs and Muslims is now sweeping the West from one end to the other. On the other side, the term 'West' is now often used in the Arab world as a comprehensive term. The western policies that backed the worst Arab dictatorships and contributed to the occupation and destruction of Iraq, where a million Iraqis have been killed on the pretext of establishing democracy, have helped to propagate the belief in the Arab world that the West is hostile to Arabs and Muslims. No one will mention that there is more to the West than western governments, and that western civilization means something other than western government policies. No one will mention that the West that produced George W. Bush and Tony Blair is the same West that produced Shakespeare, Voltaire, and Rousseau, or that the West that brought colonialism to the Arab world is the same West that provided the concepts of democracy and human rights. No one will mention the fact that the demonstrations in western capitals against invading Iraq were much larger than those in the Islamic world. Yet again the stereotype has to be final and clear-cut. What is surprising here is that the logic of extremists on both sides is completely identical. If white racists consider Arabs to be creatures who are less able and less intelligent, more violent and more bloody, many Muslim extremists think all westerners hate Islam and are conspiring against it in one way or another. The problem is mutual, so what's to be done?

I once read that during the Vietnam War the U.S. Army gave its combat troops the following order: "When you open fire, do not look the enemy in the eye." The idea is simple but deeply significant. If you look someone in the eye, you will not be able to kill him because in his eye you will see the human element. Killing is easier when we dehumanize the victim, when we think about those we kill not as human beings but as some category: Arabs, Jews, Muslims, or Hindus, or just as the enemy. I believe we all have a duty now to do the opposite of what the U.S. Army ordered. We have a duty to look each other in the eye, to communicate as humans before all else. Then we will realize that we may have different religions or skin colors but we are all fundamentally human, with the same emotions and ideas.

It is this concept that induced me to publish this book in English. A massive barrier of misunderstanding, ignorance, fear, and hatred is now going up between Arabs and westerners, and the time has come for that barrier to come down. I hope this book is a step, however small, in the right direction.

THE PRESIDENCY
AND SUCCESSION

The Egyptian Campaign against the Succession

Those who work in the theater know the moment when one scene ends, the stage goes dark, and the stage hands move in at speed to remove the set from the previous scene and replace it with the set for the next scene. This process, known as changing the set, calls for training and skill but first of all precise knowledge of what the next scene requires. Like all Egyptians I watched the latest conference of the National Democratic Party and was surprised at the extraordinary ability of the senior officials to fabricate and lie. They speak about achievements that exist only in their reports and their imaginations while millions of Egyptians live in complete misery. But I also felt that Egypt is now undergoing a 'changing the set' moment that was meant to take place quickly but has dragged on and faltered, and there are many reasons for that.

First, President Mubarak has been ruling Egypt for thirty years and is now more than eighty years old. Although I have full respect for him, by virtue of age and the law of nature he cannot continue in his position forever. A few days ago Mr. Emad Adib suddenly confronted public opinion with a most unusual remark: he said he hoped the president would give up his office and suggested presidents should be able to leave power safely, in the sense that they should not be held to account, politically or legally, for their deeds while in office. It's hard to imagine that a veteran commentator who is close to the presidency, such as Emad Adib, would venture such a precise and serious suggestion unless he had permission or instructions to do so. These signs add to the confusion on the political stage in our country, because we don't know whether the president will step down or stay in office. It often seems as though there are two wills at work at the summit of power: one in favor of the president remaining and the other in favor of him stepping down.

Second, for years the Egyptian regime has worked hard to prepare Mr. Gamal Mubarak to inherit the government of Egypt from his father. This effort has not been confined to Egypt but has extended abroad as well, and the main aim of Egyptian foreign policy is now, I'm sorry to say, to muster the support of western countries for Mr. Gamal Mubarak. The price for this western consent is the interests, the money, and the dignity of Egyptians. The Egyptian regime has understood that the key to the West's heart is in Israel's hands. If Israel is content, then all the western countries will immediately be content. For the sake of the succession the Egyptian regime has fallen over itself to offer services to Israel. From 2005 until today Israel has obtained from Egypt things it had not obtained since Camp David in 1978: the return of the Egyptian ambassador, gas, oil, and cement agreements, and, more important than all that, Egypt's attempts to persuade or force the Palestinians to do everything Israel demands. This went as far as closing the Rafah border crossing and taking part in the blockade of the Palestinians, and punishing Hamas so that it submits to Israel's will.

In return for these services the Egyptian regime has been able to obtain implicit international support on the succession question. We may recall the Sharm al-Sheikh conference that took place after the Gaza massacre, how western leaders feted President Mubarak and thanked him officially for what they called "his efforts for peace." We may also recall how President Obama, whom the American people elected to defend human rights and democracy through the world, himself heaped praise on President Mubarak as a wise leader taking steps toward democracy. This double standard has always marked the attitudes of western governments. Any allegation of electoral fraud in Iran (Israel's prime enemy) is immediately met with an intense and relentless campaign by western media and officials in defense of democracy, whereas the emergency law, detentions, torture, constitutional amendments to enable the succession, and the abolition of judicial supervision in Egypt, all that does not at all arouse the indignation of westerners, because the Egyptian regime is an important and loyal ally to Israel and the United States.

Third, the succession campaign may have succeeded internationally but inside Egypt it has been an abject failure, because Egyptians have never accepted the idea that Egypt should become a monarchical republic in which the son inherits his father's throne. Add to that the fact that Gamal Mubarak himself, while I fully respect his person, may be a successful expert on banks and business management but he does not have any political talent or experience of any kind. Dozens of meetings and seminars have been held at which Gamal Mubarak has made speeches hailed by hypocritical members of the National Democratic Party and government writers, and Mr. Gamal Mubarak has been to villages and poor neighborhoods on numerous visits where some wretched people are chosen by State Security to have their pictures taken as they clap and cheer for him. None of these campaigns has convinced Egyptians that succession is a good idea. On the contrary, they have made Egyptians reject, condemn, and sometimes joke about the succession.

Fourth, conditions in Egypt have reached rock bottom in the full sense: poverty, disease, oppression, corruption, unemployment, lack of healthcare, and deteriorating education. Would anyone have imagined that Egyptians would end up drinking sewage water? The number of people who have died on the ferry that sank, on burning trains, and in collapsed buildings is more than the number who died in all the wars Egypt has fought. That's why protests and strikes have proliferated in a way that Egypt has not seen since the revolution of 1952. The regime's apologists say these protests do not reflect a real desire for radical reform but are aimed at achieving narrow professional demands. It escapes those people that most revolutions in history started out with protest movements that did not fundamentally seek revolution, because revolution is not a slogan or a prior objective but a stage a society goes through at a certain moment, when everything becomes liable to ignite. We are definitely at such a stage. All Egyptians know that the old status quo is no longer tenable or acceptable, and that change is inevitably on its way. Our national duty is to try to ensure peaceful democratic change, or else Egypt will face the danger of overwhelming chaos, which no one wants because it would set everything ablaze.

Perhaps it is this feeling of danger that drove the great writer Mohamed Hassanein Heikal to go public with his transitional project for democratic change. Although we might not agree with some of the details of Heikal's project, it remains an excellent and objective starting point for real reform. On top of that, Egyptians have started to air the names of major figures whom they would like to see win the presidency, such as Dr. Mohamed ElBaradei, Amr Moussa, and Dr. Ahmed Zewail, all of them much more eligible than Gamal Mubarak to take on the presidency.

Lastly, a few days ago an Egyptian Campaign against Succession began, and as soon as it was announced, dozens of public figures, associations, and political parties joined it. I attended the opening meeting of this campaign and I felt optimistic at the enthusiasm and sincerity of those present. Hassan Nafaa was chosen as campaign coordinator—a respectable figure who brings great credibility to what we are doing. The members of this campaign are from diverse political trends, ranging from the Muslim Brotherhood, to socialists and Nasserists such as Abdel Halim Kandil, to liberals such as Ayman Nour and Osama al-Ghazali Harb. Despite our political and ideological differences, we have come together to perform our national duty. Our objectives are clear and legitimate: to prevent great Egypt from being passed from father to son as though it were a piece of land or a poultry farm, to restore the natural right of Egyptians to choose who rules them, and to bring about justice and freedom for Egyptians. Egypt has the potential to be a great state but this potential is thwarted by despotism. If democracy came about, Egypt would flourish within years through the work of its own people.

Dear reader, I invite you to join the Egyptian Campaign against Succession if you oppose injustice and despotism and look forward to the dignified life you and your children deserve. Come and join us. God willing, we will shape Egypt's future without waiting for them to shape it their way to serve their own interests. The time has come for us to leave our seats in the auditorium and create the next scene ourselves.

Democracy is the solution.

November 1, 2009

Three Fallacious Arguments
for Supporting Gamal Mubarak

Last week I wrote about the creation of the Egyptian Campaign against Succession, which aims to prevent President Mubarak from passing our country on to his son, Gamal, because Egypt is not a private estate or a poultry farm owned by someone, whatever his rank or position. Patriotic intellectuals, political parties, and organizations of various political and intellectual tendencies took part in setting up the campaign and all of them decided to do their best to ensure Egyptians regain their natural right to elect the next president of the republic through respectable elections.

As soon as the article appeared, dozens of messages flooded in to me from readers inside Egypt and abroad, all of them declaring their support for the campaign and asking how they can join it. I thank the readers, I appreciate their magnanimous enthusiasm, and I assure them that within a few days the campaign's founding statement will come out and the procedures for joining will be announced. We expect this campaign to enjoy complete success, God willing, but we also understand that the path will not be easy, because the Egyptian regime has formed its own special organization to promote the succession, with journalists, politicians, media people, and law professors whose sole task is to prepare the Egyptian people to accept the idea of succession. No one respects these advocates of succession because they are hypocrites who have betrayed their professional and patriotic duties, preferring to serve their personal interests over the interests of the nation. Gamal Mubarak's propagandists have only three fallacious arguments they repeat again and again. In brief, they run like this:

First, they say Mr. Gamal Mubarak is an urbane, well-educated young man and irreplaceable as the presidential candidate at this time. They also say that he will be the first civilian president of Egypt since the revolution of 1952, and that this is a step toward democracy. So why don't we all agree on him, with the provision that he promises to serve only two presidential terms? We agree with them that Gamal Mubarak is indeed urbane, has had a fair amount of education, and speaks English fluently, but we don't understand what all that has to do with the presidency. In Egypt there are hundreds of thousands of urbane people with advanced academic degrees who have good English and French. Are they all fit to be president? As for the idea that Gamal Mubarak is the only option, this is not true. Egypt has enough talent and intellectual power to serve ten countries together. As the pace of the succession process speeds up, Egyptians have started to think of major figures who would be suitable as president: Ahmed Zewail, Mohamed ElBaradei, Amr Moussa, Hesham al-Bastawisi, Zakaria Abdel Aziz, and many others. All of these are far preferable to Gamal Mubarak as president.

The argument that Gamal Mubarak will be a civilian president for Egypt is also based on a fallacy, because what defines the nature of a regime is not the profession of the president but the way in which he assumes power. There are autocratic military regimes that have put a civilian into the presidency, as happened in Syria with Bashar al-Asad, and alternatively there are democratic systems in which military men have left military service and stood for election and won, or have taken on ministerial or presidential jobs, like Colin Powell in the United States and Charles de Gaulle in France. If Gamal Mubarak gains the presidency of Egypt, this will not put an end to military rule but merely add to it another disaster. Autocracy will be combined with a hereditary system, and after that what will there be to stop Gamal Mubarak from granting the presidency to his son or nephew? Those who say that Gamal Mubarak will restrict himself to two presidential terms are trying to deceive the public and do not respect people's intelligence. What will oblige Gamal Mubarak to give up power voluntarily? At the beginning of his time in office President Hosni Mubarak also promised to restrict himself to two terms but then he went back on his promise and has stayed in power for thirty straight years.

Second, Gamal Mubarak's propagandists say that Egyptians are not interested in democracy and are not qualified to practice it because of illiteracy. They also claim that if there were free elections, the Muslim

Brotherhood would win a majority and take power. In fact Egypt is now witnessing a wave of strikes and protests on a scale unknown since the 1952 revolution. This widespread social unrest heralds change that is inevitable and not at all remote from democracy. The constant protest movements express Egyptians' demand for justice, which can come about only through democratic reform. The argument that Egyptians are not qualified for democracy, besides being insulting, reveals a shameful ignorance of Egyptian history. Democratic experiments began in Egypt earlier than in many European countries, when in 1866 Khedive Ismail set up the first advisory council of representatives. At first the council was advisory, but the members fought for and obtained real authority. From 1882 until 1952 Egyptians struggled and thousands gave their lives for two objectives: independence and the constitution. In other words freeing Egypt from British occupation was always connected in the consciousness of Egyptians with establishing democracy. Democracy means equality, justice, and freedom, and all of these are basic human rights that no one people deserves more than any other. The argument that illiteracy prevents democracy is countered by the fact that the level of illiteracy in India has not stopped a great democracy from creating a great state there in just a few years, and by the fact that the level of illiteracy before the revolution did not prevent the Wafd Party from scoring landslide victories in any free elections. The illiterate Egyptian peasants would always vote for the Wafd against the landowners, who were members of the Liberal Constitutionalist Party. No one needs a doctorate in law to know that the government of his country is oppressive and corrupt; in fact, the feelings of simple people are often closer to the truth than the views and lengthy debates of cultured people. In any case Egypt has more than forty million educated people, quite enough for a democratic experiment to succeed.

As for the Muslim Brotherhood, the Egyptian regime has exaggerated its role and influence, using it as a bogeyman to frighten western countries into agreeing to despotism and succession. The Muslim Brotherhood, in terms of numbers and influence, could not win a majority in any free elections where people turn out to vote. Even if we supposed they did win, wouldn't that be the free choice of Egyptians, which we should respect if we are true democrats? However much we may disagree with the Muslim Brotherhood, are they not in the end Egyptian citizens who have the right to win elections and take part in government as long as they respect the rules of democracy? Democratic reform alone is sure to eliminate religious extremism, whereas in autocratic countries, even if extremist movements are repressed and crushed, the causes of extremism will remain latent below the surface, awaiting the first opportunity to revive.

Last, the propagandists wonder why all these attacks are being made on Gamal Mubarak. Is he not an Egyptian citizen who has a right to stand for election to the presidency? The answer is that Gamal Mubarak will have the right to stand for the presidency only when there is a democratic system that gives all candidates equal opportunities, when the emergency law is repealed, public freedoms are granted, and the constitution is amended to allow for honest competition for the presidency, and when clean elections take place under full and independent judicial supervision, with impartial international monitoring, without intervention by the police or thugs, and without fraud. Only then will it be Gamal Mubarak's right to stand for the presidency. But for him to stand under the shadow of the current apparatus of repression and fraud would be to repeat the same wretched and ridiculous charade. He would be the nominee of the ruling National Democratic Party, the authorities would mobilize some extras from the imaginary parties invented by State Security, and then the elections would be rigged. For Gamal Mubarak to win this way would be to usurp the presidency illegally and illegitimately.

Egypt is now at a crossroads in every sense of the word. Will Egyptians, God willing, regain their right to justice and freedom, to live in their country as respected citizens who can choose, by their free and independent will, the person fit to be president of Egypt?

Democracy is the solution.

November 8, 2009

The Art of Pleasing the President

I wouldn't have believed it if I hadn't seen it myself on a tape recorded by the Mehwar channel during the recent conference of the National Democratic Party. Mrs. Suzanne Mubarak arrived in the hall surrounded by bodyguards, and ministers and officials rushed to greet her. The minister of manpower, Aisha Abdel Hady, then approached her and started to follow her. The minister was speaking about a subject that did not seem to interest Suzanne Mubarak but she kept listening with a polite smile on her face. Then suddenly, in front of everyone, including the photographers and the television cameras, Aisha Abdel Hady bent down toward Suzanne Mubarak's hand and started to kiss it. The scene looked very strange. In France, a man might kiss a woman's hand, but that custom is not widespread in Egypt. Egyptians might kiss the hand of their mother or father to express deep respect, but apart from that kissing hands in our country is considered to be incompatible with one's dignity and self-respect. In 1950 the Wafd Party had been out of power for some years and when the party was asked to form the new government, Wafd leader Mustafa al-Nahhas met King Farouk. Al-Nahhas leaned down to kiss his hand—a scandal that haunted Mustafa al-Nahhas until his death.

What would impel a government minister to bend down and kiss someone's hand? The truth is that Aisha Abdel Hady never dreamed that she would become a minister, for the simple fact that she never completed her basic education. In other words she failed to graduate from preparatory school but managed to become a minister in a country that has tens of thousands of people with doctorates. Aisha Abdel Hady understands that she was not appointed minister because of her competence or her capacity to do the job, but only because the president and his family approve of her, and in order to retain presidential approval she is fully prepared to do anything, including kissing the hands of the president, his wife, and his sons.

The question is: Can we expect Aisha Abdel Hady to defend the dignity and rights of Egyptians as she should in her role as minister of manpower? The answer is absolutely not. Thousands of Egyptians who work in the Gulf states are robbed of their due by their sponsors, are mistreated and humiliated, and are often detained and flogged unjustly. They wait for the government of their country to defend their rights, but Aisha Abdel Hady, who kisses hands, does nothing for them. On the contrary, two years ago Aisha Abdel Hady announced she had made an agreement with the Saudi authorities to provide thousands of Egyptian maids to work in Saudi homes. This extraordinary deal shocked Egyptians, first, because Egypt has hundreds of thousands of highly qualified people who are more eligible to obtain contracts to work in the Gulf; second, because sending Egyptian women to work as maids is incompatible with the most basic rules of national dignity and puts them at risk of being humiliated or sexually abused; third, because many Egyptian women have intermediate or advanced qualifications but under pressure of poverty and unemployment are forced to agree to work as maids; and, fourth, because the Saudi authorities, who are strict in all religious matters and require that women be accompanied by a close male relative when they go to the country on pilgrimage or *umra*, did the opposite this time and asked for Egyptian maids to go to Saudi Arabia unaccompanied. Aisha Abdel Hady defended the deal she made for the maids, saying there was nothing shameful about domestic service and advising her opponents to abandon their meaningless sensitivities. I remember that one Egyptian intellectual, Dr. Ayman Yahya, decided at the time to respond to the minister in a practical and inventive way. He placed an advertisement on the front page of *al-Karama* newspaper reading, "Wanted: A Saudi live-in maid for a wealthy Egyptian family. Attractive salary." He left his telephone number for people to call and over several weeks he received a barrage of curses and insults from dozens of Saudis who thought the advertisement was an affront to their country.

Under pressure of public opinion, Aisha Abdel Hady was forced to back down on sending the maids to Saudi Arabia, but she came back and announced last month that she had reached a new agreement to send Egyptian maids to Kuwait this time. I don't know why some officials in the Gulf insist on bringing maids from Egypt instead of Egyptian doctors, engineers, and other qualified Egyptian professionals of the kind who can take credit for the progress the Gulf has seen. Does using Egyptians as servants give some Gulf people a particular pleasure? I also don't understand why this strange minister is so enthusiastic about providing maids for Gulf countries. But I do understand that someone who has already lost something cannot then give it away, and someone who is willing to kiss people's hands in public cannot defend anyone's dignity. The incident when Aisha Abdel Hady kissed Suzanne Mubarak's hand reflects the relationship between the ministers and senior officials on the one hand and President Mubarak and his family on the other.

In the same tape I saw on the Mehwar channel, there are shots of Dr. Alieddin Hilal, the head of the information department at the National Democratic Party and a professor of political science, as he faced a curious dilemma when just by chance he found himself standing in the way of Mrs. Suzanne Mubarak. He was seriously confused and did not know what to do. He was worried that turning his back on her might be interpreted as an insult to her status, with serious consequences, but he dared not risk turning to her and talking to her when she had not asked him to do so. And if he decided to get out of her way suddenly, that, too, might appear as inappropriate conduct. So what should he do? The senior official looked confused and undecided. He hovered in his place until the chief bodyguard came up to him and pushed him aside so that Mrs. Suzanne Mubarak could proceed on her way. This complete submission to the president and his family is a shared characteristic of all ministers in Egypt. Perhaps readers will remember how last year Gamal Mubarak reprimanded higher education minister Hani Hilal in public at an American University in Cairo function. He prevented him from sitting next to him on the platform and with a wave of his hand told him to move away at once. The minister was not angry at the public reprimand but was merely anxious that Gamal Mubarak was angry with him.

In a democratic country a minister reaches his position through fair elections, is indebted to the voters, and does his utmost to retain their trust and their votes. If a minister there disagrees with the president he submits his resignation immediately because he knows he will regain his position if he wins in the next elections. But in a despotic system the minister does not care at all what people think because he does not obtain his position through his competence or his work, but through his loyalty to the president, and so his whole political future depends on a single word from the president. In Egypt you will never find a minister who disputes anything the president says or disagrees with him or even expresses reservations about a single word he says. They all glorify the president and praise his genius and his great achievements, which we Egyptians cannot see or feel (simply because they don't exist). Some years ago I saw a prominent state official and economist assert on television that although President Mubarak did not study economics he was gifted with an "economic inspiration," which enabled him to have brilliant and powerful economic ideas that eluded academic economists themselves. The way officials are appointed in Egypt automatically rules out qualified people, natural leaders, those who have self-respect, and those who care about their dignity, while official positions are usually given to losers, partisans, sycophants, and those who cooperate with the security agencies. This has brought conditions in Egypt to rock bottom in most fields. The moment when Aisha Abdel Hady bent down to kiss the hand of Suzanne Mubarak symbolizes how Egyptians have lost their rights at home and abroad. When there is real democratic reform, elections will bring to power competent and respectable officials who do not kiss hands and do not flatter the president and his family. Only then will Egypt prosper.

Democracy is the solution.

December 2, 2009

The Chameleons Attack ElBaradei

The story began in an ordinary way. A dog in the street attacked a passerby and bit his finger. The man shouted out in pain and people gathered around him. A policeman happened to be passing, looked into the incident, and decided he should arrest the owner of the dog and charge him with leaving his dog loose without a muzzle and putting people's lives at risk. The policeman asked whose dog it was and one of the bystanders said it belonged to the general, the governor of the city. The policeman looked embarrassed and quickly his attitude diametrically changed. Instead of talking about arresting the dog's owner, the policeman turned to the injured victim and started to tell him off. "Listen," he said. "It's a gentle creature, very docile and well-behaved. It's you who provoked it. It's you who blew smoke in its friendly face, which forced the poor dog to bite your finger in self-defense. I'm going to arrest you on a charge of provoking the dog." That's the gist of a wonderful story called *A Chameleon* by the great Russian writer, Anton Chekhov (1860–1904), and the message of the story is that some people, for the sake of their narrow little interests, change their color like chameleons and without embarrassment switch their position from one extreme to the other. I remembered this story while following the savage campaign the regime's scribes have been waging in recent days against Dr. Mohamed ElBaradei. For years this man has been the object of official honors, so much so that the Egyptian state awarded him the Nile Medal, the highest decoration in the country. At that time the regime's scribes vied to recount his virtues and accomplishments (all of them real), but as soon as Egyptians spoke out and called on ElBaradei to stand for the

15

presidency, the scribes, like the policeman in Chekhov's story, switched to the opposite extreme. They heaped curses on ElBaradei's head, and tried to minimize his importance and tarnish his reputation. Leaving aside their professional and moral degradation, there are several reasons why the regime's scribes are so terrified of Mohamed ElBaradei.

First, it's now hard for Egyptians to find a better presidential candidate than Dr. Mohamed ElBaradei, who is highly educated (a doctorate in international law from New York University) and has more international and political experience than President Hosni Mubarak had when he became president. He has widespread international connections and enjoys respect throughout the world. He has won several major international prizes besides the Nobel Peace Prize. More important than all that is the fact that in his great success ElBaradei has not depended on connections or relatives. He has proved himself by his hard work, his talent, and his dedication. That makes him a real model for millions of young people in Egypt.

Second, in all situations ElBaradei has shown that he says what he believes and does what he says. He stood alone against tremendous pressure from the United States and in 2003 issued a report in which he told the United Nations Security Council that the International Atomic Energy Agency, which he headed, had found no trace of weapons of mass destruction in Iraq, thereby removing the cover of legitimacy from the U.S. attack on Iraq. He exposed another outrage by the United States when he asked what had become of 377 tons of explosives that disappeared from Iraq after the U.S. occupation. After that he took the same honest and courageous position against war on Iran. All this made the United States strongly oppose renominating him for his post in 2005. As for Israel, it accuses him of loyalty to Arab and Islamic states.

Third, after ElBaradei reached the pinnacle of professional achievement, he could have gone into comfortable retirement and lived with honor and esteem in Egypt or abroad. He could have flattered President Mubarak with a few words, as many others do. The regime would then adore him, embrace him, and maybe give him a senior position in government. But ElBaradei showed that his love for his country and his commitment to his principles are greater than any personal considerations or interests. I have heard from witnesses how ElBaradei met senior officials of the Egyptian regime and did not hesitate to tell them what he thought of their wretched performance and how he resented the depths to which the country has sunk. Because of his attitude he was excluded after that from meeting senior officials. This moral integrity puts ElBaradei above many men in Egypt who would never dare to oppose President Mubarak or anyone from his family (even in matters of football). The fact that ElBaradei has not held any official position in Egypt for twenty years adds greatly to his credit, because he has not taken part in corruption, his hands are not soiled with dirty money, and he has not helped deceive Egyptians, rig elections, or oppress citizens. He has not been hypocritical or refrained from speaking the truth. Despite living outside Egypt he has never lost touch with the country. He follows what is happening to Egyptians and feels their suffering and problems. Suffice it to say that he donated his share of the Nobel Peace Prize, an amount of more than five million Egyptian pounds, toward the welfare of orphans in Egypt.

Fourth, something in the character of Dr. Mohamed ElBaradei makes him acceptable to Egyptians—a mixture of humility, composure, logical thinking, self-confidence, and dignity. In the minds of Egyptians ElBaradei makes a paternal impression of the kind that made them like their great leaders, men such as Saad Zaghloul, Mustafa al-Nahhas, and Gamal Abdel Nasser.

Fifth, the appearance of ElBaradei on the political scene drives the final nail into the coffin of the plan for President Mubarak to bequeath power to his son, Gamal. The 'inheritance project' depended on two ideas that have been promulgated incessantly for some years. The first is that there is no alternative to Gamal Mubarak as president of Egypt, and then suddenly ElBaradei proves that there are much better alternatives (in fact it is quite inconceivable to compare Gamal Mubarak with Mohamed ElBaradei with respect to experience and competence). The second idea, which the regime has habitually presented to western countries, is that there are only two choices in Egypt, the Mubarak regime or the Muslim Brotherhood. ElBaradei has also proved this idea to be fallacious, as a man who has won the affection and admiration of Egyptians while staying as distant as possible from both the regime and the Muslim Brotherhood.

Sixth, Mohamed ElBaradei will not easily fall prey to the Egyptian regime's usual conspiracies. The regime will not be able to frame him with a fraud charge or a sex scandal, and will not be able to throw him in jail on a charge of damaging Egypt's reputation or inciting chaos. The Egyptian regime has often used all these depraved methods to get rid of its opponents, but they will not work with ElBaradei, who already has a spotless reputation and is protected by the widespread international admiration he enjoys.

Last, just as a proficient doctor diagnoses the most serious diseases with few words, Dr. ElBaradei has managed to put his finger on the defects in the despotic regime that oppresses us. The conditions ElBaradei has set for fair presidential elections worthy of respect are exactly the steps our country has to take for the sake of a healthy democracy. ElBaradei has made it clear that he will not agree to play the role of an extra in a drama of rigged elections and has announced that he will join Egyptians in their struggle for justice and freedom. The appearance of ElBaradei is a major opportunity for all Egyptian nationalists and must not go to waste. We must join Dr. Mohamed ElBaradei in defending the usurped rights of Egyptians. Dr. Mohamed ElBaradei is expected to arrive in Egypt on January 15 and we all have a duty to welcome this great man with all the honor and esteem he deserves. We want to show him that his inspiring message has reached us, that we love and respect him, and that with him we will do our utmost to bring about a renaissance in Egypt and give the country the status it deserves.

Democracy is the solution.

December 13, 2009

Should Gaza Pay the Price for Hereditary
Succession in Egypt?

S ince the Israeli newspaper *Haaretz* published the news and the
United States administration confirmed it, the Egyptian government has finally admitted it is building a steel wall underground
along the border with Gaza to close down the tunnels Palestinians use to
smuggle in food and medicine. The smuggling is in response to the crippling blockade Israel has imposed on the Gaza Strip for more than two
years, to which Egypt has contributed by closing the Rafah border crossing to Palestinians. We have several observations to make:

First, the aim of the blockade, as announced by Israel, is to wipe out
the Palestinian resistance and starve the people of Gaza until they submit to Israel and accept Israel's conditions for a final peace settlement in
which the Palestinians would lose their rights forever. But the legendary
resistance of the Palestinians drove Israel to commit a brutal massacre
in which it used weapons prohibited internationally and in which more
than 1,400 people lost their lives, at least half of them women and children. In spite of the massacre and the blockade the Palestinians have
not capitulated but have continued to resist valiantly, driving Israel to
think of a way to strangle them once and for all. It is certain that the
underground steel wall is basically an Israeli idea that the Egyptian government was reluctant to implement. But Egypt then agreed and began
to build the wall, which is being constructed with American financing
and under American supervision. The purpose of the wall is to kill
the Palestinians literally, because it will eliminate their last chance for
obtaining food.

Second, by closing the Rafah border crossing, thereby preventing Arab and international relief convoys from reaching Gaza, and then by building the steel wall to starve the Palestinians, the Egyptian government is regrettably committing heinous crimes against our brothers as Arabs and as fellow humans. Arab solidarity and Egypt's duty toward the Muslims and Christians in Palestine are no longer considerations that count for anything for Egyptian officials, who openly ridicule them. But the Egyptian regime, in its enthusiasm to please Israel, has not taken into account that it is tarnishing its own reputation throughout the world. The Gaza massacre a year ago has already destroyed what remains of Israel's international reputation and the voices of condemnation have grown louder in western countries to an unprecedented extent. In October, former Israeli Prime Minister Ehud Olmert went to make a speech at the University of Chicago and found himself surrounded by students shouting in his face, "Butcher of Gaza . . . child-killer." Several western judges have issued warrants against Israeli leaders to answer charges of committing war crimes in Gaza and Lebanon. This has happened in Belgium, Norway, Spain, and recently Britain, where the British police were about to arrest former Israeli Foreign Minister Tzipi Livni, who escaped at the last minute. It is true that most of these warrants were withdrawn because of massive Zionist pressure on western governments, but they clearly demonstrate an international mood of condemnation toward Israel that never existed in the past. The Egyptian regime, by building the wall, is not only risking its popularity in Egypt and the Arab world, which is already at rock bottom, but also staining its reputation worldwide.

Third, all the excuses the regime presents to justify building the wall would not convince a small child. It says that Egypt is free to build the wall as long as it is inside Egyptian territory, overlooking the fact that the freedom of any state, by custom, logic, and international law, is not absolute but restricted by the rights of others, and that Egypt cannot be instrumental in starving one and a half million human beings who live next door and then claim it is free to do as it likes. The regime says the tunnels are used for smuggling weapons to terrorists in Egypt. We say that weapons have been smuggled in from Libya and Sudan, so does the Egyptian government intend to build steel walls along its borders with all neighboring countries? If the Ministry of Interior, with its massive security apparatus, is unable to protect the borders, then what is it doing with the eight billion Egyptian pounds a year in budget money it receives from the Egyptian people?

The regime is now using the slogan, "Egyptian national security is a red line." We believe in this slogan and do not contest it, but national security in our opinion starts by defining who is Egypt's enemy. Is it Israel or the people of Gaza? If Israel is our enemy—and that is the truth— would it not be in Egypt's national interest to support the Palestinian resistance? Didn't anyone wonder why the Palestinians are compelled to dig tunnels underground? It has been the only way for them to survive. Would the Palestinians be digging tunnels if Egypt opened the Rafah crossing and allowed food and medicine to reach them? When Egypt builds this wall to starve Palestinians to death, should we blame Palestinians if they use force to stop its construction or try to destroy it? Or isn't that legitimate self-defense? The officials speak much about the Egyptian officer who was shot and killed with a bullet fired from Gaza, and we, too, greatly regret the death of that martyr, but we also remember that there is not one piece of evidence that the bullet came from the Hamas movement and we remember that Israel by its own admission has killed several Egyptian officers and troops on the border. Why wasn't our government angry for the sake of national security then? And where was this national security when the Israelis admitted to killing hundreds of Egyptians and burying them in mass graves during war, and officials in Egypt did not take a single measure against the Israeli war criminals? Officials in Egypt say they have closed the Rafah border crossing for fear of a mass influx of Palestinians into Egypt, but this is a foolish argument because what drove the Palestinians to break through the crossing was their pressing need for food. They bought with their own money what they needed from Egyptian traders and then went back where they came from. So what do we expect from the Palestinians after we shut off, with the steel wall, their last chance to live? Would anyone blame them if they poured across by the thousands, breaking through the Rafah crossing by force to escape death by starvation? This wall, besides being a heinous act and an indelible mark of shame on the brow of the Egyptian government, constitutes a real threat to Egyptian national security.

Fourth, what is driving the Egyptian regime to all this submission to Israeli policy? One factor is that the regime believes any victory for Hamas would help the Muslim Brotherhood and that this would threaten the Egyptian government. This is a big mistake, because victory for the resistance would greatly help Egypt and would not at all pose a threat to it. Besides, the Muslim Brotherhood, with its size and influence, is not a real threat to the Egyptian regime, which always promulgates that theory in order to justify despotism. The second factor is that the Egyptian regime knows that fulfilling Israel's desires is the sure path to American approval. In the last few years Israel has obtained from Egypt more than it obtained after the Camp David agreements were signed: the release of the spy Azam Azam, agreements to sell gas and cement, the blockade of the Palestinians, and finally this disgraceful wall. That explains America's satisfaction with the Mubarak regime. A few days ago the U.S. ambassador in Cairo, Margaret Scobey, said she thought that democracy in Egypt was going well. This bizarre statement shows us the extent to which the Zionist lobby controls U.S. policy. The United States will remain satisfied with the despotic regime in Egypt as long as Israel is satisfied with it. After that, can Ms. Scobey wonder why Egyptians hate U.S. policy and accuse the United States of hypocrisy and double standards?

Finally, the crime of building the wall to starve the Palestinians is not unconnected with the question of democratic reform in Egypt, since the regime agreed to build the wall because it needs U.S. support for its plan to have President Mubarak pass on the presidency to his son, Gamal. Here we see a dangerous example of the consequences of despotic rule. The interests of the regime in Egypt have truly become contrary to the interests of the Egyptian people. If the Mubarak regime were democratic it would never dare to take part in the blockade and starvation of the Palestinians. Democratic systems alone are the ones whose interests are at one with those of the people and the nation.

Democracy is the solution.

December 27, 2009

Why Are We Falling Behind
as the World Progresses?

A few months ago scientist Ahmed Zewail was appointed scientific adviser to United States President Barack Obama, and when Dr. Zewail went to meet President Obama White House officials gave him an entry pass stating his name and his position, but he noticed that at the bottom of the pass they had written the word "temporary." Surprised at this, the scientist went to a senior White House official and asked, "Why have they written the word 'temporary' on my pass?"

The official smiled and said, "Dr. Zewail, you're working as an adviser to President Obama, aren't you?"

"Yes."

"President Obama himself is temporary," the official said.

When Dr. Zewail told me of this incident, I thought it significant in several ways. The U.S. president, like the president in any democratic country, holds office for four years, extendable to eight if he is reelected, after which he cannot remain in office a single day longer. The president obtained office because the people chose him of their own free will, and he is liable to strict oversight in everything related to himself and his family. Because he owes his office to the public and is liable to oversight by the people, he does his best to fulfill the promises on the basis of which the electors voted for him. This necessarily impels him to seek out the most competent people in the country to benefit from them in serving the people. That's what happens in democratic countries, whereas we in Egypt have a president who holds on to power until his inevitable end overtakes him—a practice that definitely has serious repercussions, whoever the president may be and however good his intentions.

First, the president in Egypt does not take office through voters' choice but through the power of the security agencies and their ability to suppress opponents, so he does not attach much weight to public opinion, knowing that his survival in office does not depend on people liking him but rather on the ability of the security agencies to protect him from any rebellion or coup. The security agencies in Egypt are the authority that has the decisive say in every sphere and in every detail, starting with the appointment of the mayor in the smallest village to the appointment of deans of faculties and university presidents, and even allowing political parties to be formed, granting licenses to newspapers and satellite channels, and appointing and disqualifying people for ministerial positions. So many competent people have been candidates for ministerial office but were immediately disqualified when the security agencies objected to them. And so many incompetent people have been elevated to senior positions thanks to support from the security agencies. Among the countries of the world Egypt is in a uniquely abnormal situation: the state spends nearly 9 billion Egyptian pounds a year on the Ministry of Interior, twice the budget of the Ministry of Health (which is less than 5 billion pounds a year). In other words the Egyptian regime spends twice as much on subjugating, detaining, and repressing Egyptians as it spends on providing them with healthcare.

Second, there is no legitimate way to compete with the president for office and the supreme objective is to ensure that the current president stays in power. That's why, if any public figure surfaces who enjoys the people's confidence, the regime gets upset and endeavors to get rid of him as soon as possible. This has always meant Egypt is deprived of major talents who are excluded because they have qualities that might make them eligible, even notionally, to assume the presidency. What happened to Dr. Zewail himself is the best example of that: after winning the Nobel Prize for Chemistry he returned to Egypt to submit a project for a technological university that could help move the country into the scientific age. But rumors and security reports warned that he was immensely popular among young people, many of whom said they wished to see Ahmed Zewail become president of Egypt. That was the death knell. The regime blocked every path in the face of Dr. Zewail, started to harass him, and lost interest in the university project he had hoped would benefit the country. A few months later the U.S. president quickly appointed him as his scientific adviser to benefit from his rich knowledge. Dr. Zewail is one example of the thousands of outstanding Egyptians who cannot contribute their talents because of despotism.

Third, in Egypt the president has absolute powers and no authority can hold him to account. We have no idea how large President Mubarak's fortune is or how much money his sons, Gamal and Alaa, have in the bank. What is the budget of the presidency and how does it break down into categories of spending? Is it proper that the state should spend millions of pounds of public money on the president's rest houses and palaces while millions of Egyptians live in wretched shantytowns without basic human necessities? The president's complete immunity from accountability also extends to senior officials. Audit departments in Egypt go after junior civil servants, hold them to account for the slightest lapse, and often bring about their dismissal and imprisonment. But faced with senior officials their authority is weak; they merely submit details of any transgressions to the president, and it is up to him alone whether he wants to hold them to account or turn a blind eye to their transgressions. In this way enforcement of the law is confined to the small, the weak, and senior people who have fallen out of favor. To fight corruption selectively, besides being meaningless and ineffective, is in itself a form of corruption.

Fourth, in Egypt the president has the authority to appoint and dismiss ministers. He does not consider himself responsible for explaining his decisions to Egyptians, who never know why ministers are appointed or dismissed. And competence is not the prime factor in choosing ministers, as it is loyalty to the president that is most important. Last week we saw how Ahmed Zaki Badr was appointed minister of education although he has no accomplishments to his name and has no experience of improving education. His sole achievement when he was president of Ain Shams University is, in short, that for the first time in the history of Egyptian universities he called groups of thugs armed with knives and petrol bombs onto the university campus and allowed them to attack protesting students. This disgraceful behavior, which in any democratic country would have ensured the dismissal and immediate trial of a university president, was apparently the motive for Ahmed Zaki Badr's appointment as minister of education.

On top of this, the appointment and replacement of ministers generally takes place for subjective reasons no one understands. So the prime minister, who holds the highest political office after the president, is someone who has never in his life engaged in politics; the minister of social solidarity was originally responsible for the postal authority; the minister of information was originally a specialist in selling scientific encyclopedias; and former housing minister Mohamed Ibrahim Suleiman was appointed by presidential decree to be the chairman of an oil company. It appears that the president likes some officials and trusts their loyalty, shuffling the top positions among them without thinking too much about their suitability or experience. The regime excludes major talents because it doubts their loyalty or fears their popularity, whereas it grants positions to followers, even if they are incompetent. Because most members of parliament belong to the ruling party and have won their seats through rigged elections, they carry out the government's instructions instead of playing their supervisory role. In Egypt a minister does not consider himself responsible to the people and knows full well that his survival in office does not depend on what he achieves but on whether he pleases the president. Now we can understand why ministers fall over each other to extol the president, laud his wisdom, and sing the praises of his amazing and historic decisions. Even the minister of manpower, Aisha Abdel Hady, had not the slightest qualms about bending down in public and in front of the media to kiss the hand of Mrs. Suzanne Mubarak.

For all these reasons we are falling behind day by day as the world around us is progressing. Egypt has millions of educated people and thousands of honest people with rare talents who, if given a chance, are quite capable of bringing about a major renaissance within a few years. But despotism is the fundamental reason why Egypt and Egyptians are falling behind.

Democracy is the solution.

January 17, 2010

The Only Way to Evict Mr. Battista

Dr. Galal Amin lives with his English wife, Jan, and his children in an elegant house surrounded by a beautiful garden in the suburb of Maadi. In the summer of 1971, Dr. Amin decided to go to Beirut with his family on a one-year assignment. He had the idea to rent his house and he easily found a tenant—a diplomat from Panama by the name of Mr. Battista. Dr. Amin signed a lease with him for just one year. Battista could live in the house for the year and was expected to leave when the lease expired. Matters proceeded normally but Dr. Amin came back to Egypt at the end of the year to find a surprise awaiting him. Mr. Battista refused to leave the house, arguing that Dr. Amin had not given him notice by registered letter, as the contract required. Dr. Amin tried to convince Battista that he had agreed from the start to lease the house for one year, without the possibility of renewal, and reminded him that he had telephoned him before the lease expired in what amounted to friendly notice that he should leave the house. But Battista requested one postponement after another, kept prevaricating and equivocating about when he would leave, and in the end openly declared he would not leave the house. Dr. Amin had to rent a furnished flat where he lived with his family, but a sense of injustice weighed on him until it became a violent rage.

On Christmas Eve Dr. Amin said to his wife, "Tomorrow we're going to spend the night at our house." Throughout the night Dr. Amin made calls to the tenant's number and then hung up on him without saying a word. He did this dozens of times, depriving Battista of sleep and also putting his nerves on edge. Early the next morning, Dr. Amin hired three carts and put his bags and furniture on them, then knocked on the door

27

of the house. Battista came out and Dr. Amin asked him to vacate the house immediately. Battista pretended to agree, but he lured Dr. Amin to the veranda and then locked all the doors from the inside. Dr. Amin went to his car and brought a steel jack crank and without hesitation smashed the glass doors of the house. The glass flew everywhere and Dr. Amin had cuts that bled until his face and his clothes were covered in blood. But he broke into the house nonetheless and took his bags in without any resistance from Battista, who was terrified at what was happening. Dr. Amin's wife came and took him to the hospital, where his injuries were bandaged up. Then he went back to the house with bandages on his face. He went inside, lay down on his bed, and told Battista that he must leave immediately.

Battista called the police and the police officer tried to settle the matter amicably. Battista asked for another delay but Dr. Amin refused and insisted he leave the house at once. He said he was prepared to pay in full for Battista to stay in any hotel until he could find other accommodation. At that stage Battista brought up the contract as an argument and gave it to the officer. Dr. Amin then asked to see the contract, took it from the officer, tore it to pieces, and threw the pieces on the floor. The officer was furious with Dr. Amin and went off threatening to take the matter to the highest level. But Dr. Amin, who had prepared for battle by making contact with all the officials he knew, took no notice. He remained lying in bed, despite his injuries, his exhaustion, and the bandages covering his face. At that point Battista realized that he had to give way. He packed up his belongings and walked out of the house, leaving it to its owners.

I read of this incident in the classic book al-Shorouk recently published, the second part of Galal Amin's autobiography and an exquisite contribution to Arabic literature. As I read what Dr. Amin did with Battista, I was surprised, first, because Galal Amin is one of the greatest and most important Arab intellectuals and, second, because I know him well, for he has been my friend and my mentor for twenty years, and he is certainly one of the most gentle and modest men I know. How could matters come to such a pass that he would behave in this violent manner? The reason is that Dr. Amin realized that this was the only way to recover his house from occupation. He had spoken amicably with Battista often and repeatedly and had given him one postponement after another, but Battista refused to leave. Recourse to legal procedures was bound to waste years before Galal Amin won his rights.

I can't help but compare what happened in Galal Amin's house and what is happening in Egypt as a whole. The regime that governs Egypt, just like Battista the tenant, has kept an illegitimate grip on power for thirty years through repression and fraud. For years we have been asking the regime to grant Egyptians their natural right to choose those who govern them and, just like Battista, the regime prevaricates and equivocates in order to retain its monopoly on power, and is even trying to pass it on from President Mubarak to his son, Gamal, after him. Because of despotism and corruption, conditions in Egypt in every field have sunk to rock bottom. Millions of Egyptians suffer from poverty and unemployment and live in conditions unfit for human beings. Every day there are more and more strikes and sit-ins, as though every sector of society is protesting against what is happening.

Question: Given this widespread and growing anger, why is change taking so long? The answer is that Egyptians need to understand, like Galal Amin, that rights are not bestowed but have to be wrested, and that at a certain moment the injured party has to summon up his resolve to obtain his rights, whatever sacrifices he has to make. I am not calling for violence. I am calling for pressure by all peaceful means to wrest back the usurped rights of Egyptians. Egypt is now at a real turning point and more ripe for change than at any time in the past. Egyptians felt great hope when Dr. Mohamed ElBaradei appeared and announced he was joining a national effort to bring about democracy and social justice. I have met Dr. ElBaradei in person and my admiration for him has grown. From up close I sensed ElBaradei's humility, sincerity, balanced thinking, and deep feeling for the suffering of Egyptians. What matters to Dr. ElBaradei is not standing for the presidency, because he is a person very far from liking power and because his professional and social status make it superfluous to him. Besides, if ElBaradei or anyone else stood for the presidency under the current flawed constitution, which restricts the post to the president and his sons, any candidate would in effect be a trifling extra in the drama of the presidential succession, and that would be a disgrace Dr. ElBaradei and anyone with any self-respect could not accept. ElBaradei's only cause is reform and his hope is to see his country in the place it deserves. A few days ago he announced the creation of the National Association for Change and called on all Egyptians to join. The aims of this association are to abolish the emergency law, to hold clean and respectable elections under full judicial supervision and international monitoring, and to amend the constitution to allow for equal and fair opportunities to compete for the presidency.

The approach ElBaradei advocates deems democratic reform to be the only way toward economic reform and achieving social justice. It is truly gladdening that Dr. ElBaradei's popularity is growing daily in a manner without precedent. Tens of thousands of Egyptians have declared they support ElBaradei and have full trust in him, and the signature campaign will continue until a million Egyptians have signed. Then we have to move to the confrontation stage. It's no longer any use begging for our rights by appealing to the regime, because it will not listen. But if a million Egyptians went out to the streets in protest or announced a general strike, if that happened, even once, the regime would immediately heed the people's demands. Change, as far as it goes, is possible and imminent, but there is a price we have to pay for it. We will not triumph in the battle for change unless we summon up our resolve to recover our rights, whatever the sacrifices might be. It's the only way to evict Battista.

Democracy is the solution.

February 28, 2010

What Do Egyptians Expect
from ElBaradei?

The political system in Egypt is facing a veritable crisis because President Mubarak (to whom we wish a speedy recovery) may have to retire at any moment and because the regime, despite its great efforts to market Gamal Mubarak, has completely failed to convince Egyptians that the son is worthy of the presidency. On top of that, most Egyptians fundamentally reject the idea of hereditary succession, whether for Gamal Mubarak or anyone else, and insist on their natural right to choose their rulers. At the same time Dr. Mohamed ElBaradei has succeeded in portraying himself as a real leader for Egyptians in the battle for change. The broad popular support ElBaradei now enjoys is a rare political phenomenon seen only a few times in our history, with Saad Zaghloul, Gamal Abdel Nasser, and Mustafa al-Nahhas. Egyptians from various intellectual and political trends have come together in support of ElBaradei—Islamists, Copts, socialists, liberals, Nasserists, Wafdists, and, most important of all, millions of ordinary Egyptians who have seen in ElBaradei a leader who embodies their dreams of justice and freedom. Given the crisis in the system and the widespread support for ElBaradei, it might be useful for us to ask what Egyptians expect from ElBaradei. In brief the answer is as follows:

First, Dr. ElBaradei held a senior international position as director general of the International Atomic Energy Agency and such people do not stop working when they retire from so high a position. As soon as they leave their posts they receive a barrage of invitations to give lectures and take part in various international activities. Egyptians expect that

Dr. ElBaradei will eventually settle in Egypt and give priority to leading a national campaign, because a leader who defends the rights of the nation must always remain on the field of battle. I trust that Dr. ElBaradei will remember what Mustafa al-Nahhas did when he took over the leadership of the Wafd Party in 1927. At the time he was a big well-known lawyer but as soon as he became party leader he withdrew from legal practice, closed his office, and made his famous remark: "Today I have become an advocate for the whole nation, so I can no longer defend individuals in court."

Second, before the appearance of ElBaradei several national movements for change had sprung up, the most important of which was the Kefaya movement, which deserves most of the credit for breaking the barrier of fear for Egyptians. The Kefaya members who defied the emergency law, who were hit on the head by riot police, and who put up with detention and torture are the ones who won back for the whole nation the right to demonstrate and go on strike. They are the true fathers of the protest movements that have now proliferated from one end of Egypt to the other, although all movements for change in Egypt, including the Kefaya movement, have suffered from having weak links with the broad masses of Egyptians. But in ElBaradei's case the opposite has happened. ElBaradei's popularity began in the street and then moved to the elite. The people who made ElBaradei popular are not big intellectuals and politicians, but the tens of thousands of ordinary Egyptians who like him and trust him. This widespread popular support for ElBaradei imposes on him an obligation to remain always among the people. Dr. ElBaradei's entourage now includes some of the best and most sincere Egyptian nationalists, but the door must remain open to all. Dr. ElBaradei has become a leader for all Egyptians, whatever their political inclination, so any Egyptian has the right to meet Dr. ElBaradei and convey his or her ideas to him and Dr. ElBaradei has a duty to listen. Dr. ElBaradei's success in his enormous task will always remain dependent on keeping in touch with ordinary simple people.

Third, by announcing the formation of the National Association for Change, Dr. ElBaradei made a shrewd political move, and I expect that hundreds of thousands, maybe millions, of Egyptians will join this association, though it is not yet open for membership. People in Egypt and abroad want to join ElBaradei but they do not know what to do. They must be given more of a chance to take part, beyond writing the endorsements now being collected. The broad support ElBaradei enjoys has gathered around him a group of the best minds and talents in Egypt, and they are all looking forward to the moment when they will be called on to perform any mission for the sake of their country. We expect Dr. ElBaradei, as soon as he returns from abroad, quickly to choose a headquarters for the association, start enrolling members, and set up specialist committees to take advantage of all this talent in order to achieve the reform we all desire.

Fourth, we expect Dr. ElBaradei to be ready for violent confrontation with the current regime. ElBaradei has gone beyond the role of political reformer to the role of political leader, and it would be natural for the despotic regime to defend its privileges with great ferocity. So there is no point in avoiding or postponing confrontation because it is inevitable. It has already started: as in the last week one of ElBaradei's supporters, Dr. Taha Abdel Tawab, was summoned to the State Security Prosecution headquarters in the province of Fayoum, where he was stripped, beaten, tortured, and humiliated in a horrendous and inhumane manner. This crime, which takes place daily in State Security offices, takes on new significance this time. It is a message from the regime to those who demand change that no one is immune from abuse by the authorities even if they enjoy a high position in society. Dr. ElBaradei is aware of that and when he was in Korea he issued a press statement strongly condemning the assault on Dr. Taha Abdel Tawab and declaring his full solidarity. But this horrendous incident is just the beginning of the war against ElBaradei, a war in which the regime will use every weapon, legitimate and illegitimate, in order to eliminate Egyptians' hopes of freedom. We expect Dr. ElBaradei to use his extensive experience of international law to prosecute the executioners who detain the innocent and use torture, and bring them to trial before international courts.

Fifth, from the start Dr. ElBaradei has firmly refused to be a presidential candidate through one of the recognized political parties. He has also refused to submit an application to form a new party to the Parties Committee. Last week news leaked about a secret deal between the regime, the Tagammu and Wafd Parties, and the Muslim Brotherhood by which they would refrain from supporting ElBaradei in exchange for some seats in the People's Assembly in the next rigged elections. This unfortunate deal shows the level to which some politicians in Egypt have sunk, but it equally proves to us how wise and far-sighted ElBaradei was when he refused to deal with them. This has enabled him to retain his clean image among the public, away from the corruption of the regime and of those who pretend to oppose it while in secret colluding with the regime against the rights of the people. Egyptians look forward to Dr. ElBaradei sticking to his principled position, rejecting any kind of negotiation or compromises. What Egyptians are asking for is not a limited adjustment in policies but comprehensive, radical reform. Every Egyptian who signs an endorsement for ElBaradei and for changing the constitution is at the same time saying he or she is withdrawing confidence from the current system. So there is no point in appeals and in composing petitions, because rights are not granted but won. Our ability to bring about justice is always tied to our willingness to make sacrifices for its sake. A hundred eloquent petitions to the regime will not convince officials of the virtues of democracy, but if a million demonstrators went out on the streets . . . only then would the regime find itself finally forced to answer demands for reform.

While all Egypt awaits the return of Dr. ElBaradei from his trip abroad, I thought it my duty to convey to him what is going through the minds of the Egyptians who love him, have pinned great hopes on him, and are fully confident—as I am—that Mohamed ElBaradei will never let them down.

Democracy is the solution.

March 15, 2010

When Will President Mubarak
Grasp This Truth?

Mohamed Reza Pahlavi, the late shah of Iran, ruled the country from 1941 until 1979 and had close ties to British and United States intelligence, to whom he owed his restoration to the throne after his prime minister, nationalist leader Mohamed Mosaddegh, forced him into exile in 1953. The shah ruled through violent repression of his opponents, and the Iranian secret police, SAVAK, was responsible for killing or torturing hundreds of thousands of Iranians in the years before the Iranian revolution in 1979. By any impartial and objective standards, the shah of Iran was a vicious dictator whose hands were stained with the blood of Iranians, and a pawn, in the literal sense of the word, of the United States and the West. Two years ago I met his widow, Farah Pahlavi, at the home of some mutual friends in Cairo. I was impressed by her open, pleasant, and modest personality and struck by her sharp intelligence and superior education. We had a long talk and she told me she was writing her memoirs, and promised to give me a copy when they came out. She did send me a copy recently, published by al-Shorouk. When I started reading them, I was taken aback to discover that the former empress of Iran sees the late shah as a national hero who brought great benefits to Iran, and that she views the Iranian revolution as just a conspiracy by a bunch of riffraff and malcontents. Describing the last moments before the revolution forced her and her husband to leave Iran, she writes, "We were leaving with heads held high, sure of having worked ceaselessly for the benefit of the country. And if we had made mistakes, at least we had never thought of anything but the general good." I was surprised at what she said and wondered how this cultured and intelligent woman could ignore or overlook the horrendous crimes the shah committed against his country. It may be that a wife's love for her husband always blinds her to his faults, but here we are not talking about personal flaws but horrific crimes against millions of Iranians. It is even stranger that the memoirs are full of indications that the shah of Iran himself believed that he had done his country great favors, sacrificing his comfort and his life for the sake of the country.

That leads to the question: How do autocratic rulers in general see themselves? History teaches us that all autocratic rulers consider themselves great heroes and live in such a state of perpetual self-delusion that they are able to justify all their misconduct and even the crimes they perpetrate. This constant dissociation between the autocratic ruler and what happens in reality is a phenomenon that has been carefully described in international literature and is known as 'dictator's solitude.' The dictator lives in complete isolation from the lives of his compatriots and does not know what is really happening in his country. After he has been in power for years, a group of friends and rich relatives forms around him and their extravagant lifestyle keeps them apart from the way of life of ordinary people, and so the dictator loses any awareness of the poor and has absolutely no contact with real life. An image of it is conveyed to him in reports by various security agencies, but these agencies always think it is in their interest to put a gloss on the bleak reality to avoid angering the dictator. They often compete with each other for the trust of the dictator and write conflicting reports. Sometimes they make up imaginary conspiracies they claim to have thwarted in order to convince the ruler of their importance. On top of that, the ministers who work with the dictator are not elected and hence have no interest in what people think of them. Their only concern is to retain the approval of the ruler who appointed them and who can dismiss them at any moment. They never confront the ruler with the truth, but always tell him what he would like to hear. In an autocratic system the ministers rarely venture to express their real opinions; they merely await the president's instructions and they consider that whatever the president does or says or even thinks is the height of wisdom, courage, and greatness.

In this way the dictator becomes completely isolated from reality until one day he wakes up when disaster befalls the country or a revolution overthrows him. 'Dictator's solitude' is a phenomenon that recurs through history and it is one of the worst defects of an autocratic system. When the French revolution broke out in 1789 and mobs, angry and hungry, surrounded the palace of Versailles, Queen Marie Antoinette of France allegedly asked why they were demonstrating. When one of her aides told her they were angry because they could not find bread, the queen is said to have replied in surprise: "Let them eat cake." This famous remark attributed to Marie Antoinette shows how isolated an autocratic ruler can become. Marie Antoinette was a strong and intelligent woman and in fact was the real power behind the decisions taken by her husband, King Louis XVI, but after years of autocracy she was living in a different and remote world.

I thought about this while following what was happening in Egypt when President Mubarak went to have surgery in Germany. Of course I wish everyone who is sick a speedy recovery but I do not think that the president's illness is particularly special. Everyone falls ill and the president's advanced age is bound to bring some health problems from time to time. But the regime's scribes treated the president's illness as though it were the end of the world and some of them even wrote that the country itself had fallen ill with the same disease, as if President Mubarak was the incarnation and embodiment of all Egypt. This cheap and disgraceful sycophancy continued throughout the time he was under treatment, and when the surgery was successful and President Mubarak came back to Egypt, the sycophants let loose with their chorus of pipes and drums. Some singers received orders to compose songs specifically to celebrate the president's auspicious return. I don't know how any real artist could allow himself to sing eulogies for a fee, like those beggars who go around the annual festivals of popular holy men. Have these sycophants thought what they will do when the president goes to Germany again for further treatment? Will they compose new songs for when he returns? Does President Mubarak believe this flattery? Does it ever occur to him, even for a moment, that these pipers and drummers don't like him, but are merely defending the privileges they have acquired under his rule? Doesn't President Mubarak realize that these sycophants have always clung to those in power and have shaped their own ideas and opinions to be in tune with the ruler? They were loyal socialists in the time of President Gamal Abdel Nasser, but when the wind changed and the state turned to the market economy they become some of the prime advocates of privatization and the free market.

What conception of what is happening in Egypt does President Mubarak have? Does he know that more than half of all Egyptians live below the poverty line? Does it bother the president that millions of Egyptians live in shantytowns without water, electricity, or a sewage system? Is he upset at the prevalence of unemployment, poverty, disease, and frustration? Does President Mubarak know that Egypt has hit rock bottom in many fields? Has he heard about the poor people who die standing in line to obtain bread or cooking gas? Has he heard of the death boats on which thousands of young Egyptians embark to escape misery, only to drown on the high seas? Has anyone told the president that for months thousands of civil servants and their children have been lying on the pavement in front of parliament because their lives are no longer tolerable? Has President Mubarak thought about civil servants who support a whole family on a salary of 100 Egyptian pounds ($18) a month when the price of meat has risen to 70 pounds a kilo? Of course I don't know how President Mubarak thinks, though I imagine, based on the theory of 'dictator's solitude,' that his conceptions are completely detached from the reality of what is happening in Egypt. The reality is liable to produce an explosion at any moment, and if that explosion takes place, God forbid, we will all pay a heavy price. I hope President Mubarak ends his many years in office by carrying out real democratic reform, amending the constitution to allow for honest competition between candidates and for free and fair elections so that Egyptians can choose new faces—people who are respected and willing to take responsibility for ending the ordeal Egypt has been through and to begin a new future. When will President Mubarak grasp this truth?

Democracy is the solution.

April 6, 2010

Does Rigging Elections Count
as a Major Sin?

Over the coming eighteen months or so Egypt will have parliamentary and then presidential elections. In the past the Egyptian regime has tried to use judges to conceal election rigging, but upright judges refused to betray their principles and their message was clear: "Either we supervise the elections seriously and scrupulously, or we'll withdraw and let the regime alone take responsibility for the fraud." This time the regime has decided from the start to abolish judicial supervision and has announced that it will not allow any international monitoring of the voting. All this confirms that the next elections will be rigged. Even now Egyptians are well aware that members of the ruling party will win the majority of seats in parliament and that the presidential elections next year will be a farce through which President Mubarak will either hang on to power or bequeath it to his son, Gamal.

The question here is: Who is responsible for rigging elections? The Ministry of Interior is the authority that supervises the conduct of elections and so is responsible for rigging them, but in fact the interior minister is no more than carrying out orders. The person who takes the decision to rig elections is the president himself, and so the decision to rig is conveyed from the president to the interior minister and is then implemented by thousands of police officers and civil servants across the country. These are the people who prevent people from voting, call in thugs to beat up voters who don't belong to the ruling party, fill in unused ballot papers, close the ballot boxes, and then announce fabricated election results. These fraudsters, like most Egyptians these days, are conscientious about performing their prayers, fasting in Ramadan, giving alms, and going on pilgrimage, and they ask their wives and daughters to wear the *hijab*. Although they are meticulous about these religious obligations, they take part in election rigging and do not in the least feel they are committing a religious sin. They are not kept awake at night by any feelings of guilt. Generally they consider themselves merely to be carrying out the orders of their bosses, as though they see the whole question of elections as unconnected with religion.

Let's imagine, for example, that the president, instead of giving orders to rig elections, gave the police and civil servants orders to drink alcohol or not to fast in Ramadan. They would definitely rise up against him and refuse to carry out his orders, on the grounds that one must not obey a human being if it means disobeying God. Why do these civil servants see rigging elections as just carrying out orders when they see drinking alcohol and failing to fast in Ramadan as serious sins? The answer will lead us to comprehend the vast gap between the reality of Islam and the way we understand it. Pick any book you like on Islamic law and you will not find in it a single word on rigging elections, because they are all old books written in ages when elections were unknown. The gate of *ijtihad*, or individual judgment in matters of Islamic law, was closed centuries ago, and most experts in Islamic law now do no more than recapitulate legal opinions pronounced a thousand years ago. Besides, many jurists in Islamic history allied themselves with despotic rulers, and while they did explain the Islamic precepts on many aspects of life, they deliberately ignored the political rights of Muslims. In fact some of them distorted the truth and interpreted religion in a way designed to prop up the despot and exempt him from any oversight.

In Egypt there are dozens of famous sheikhs attached to various religious schools, from the sheikhs at al-Azhar, to the Salafi sheikhs, to new preachers, and every day they preach to Egyptians in thousands of mosques and on dozens of satellite channels, dealing with everything in the life of a Muslim—marriage and divorce, whether to wear gold or silk, even how to perform the ritual ablution to remove a serious impurity—but none of them ever says a single word about rigging elections. A few months ago I met a famous new preacher and found him to be a cultured young man. He asked to attend the weekly salon I organize and I welcomed him. When he came he found the audience talking about democracy and the emergency law and asserting that Egyptians have the right to choose their rulers. He did not contribute a single word to the discussion but sat in silence and then left. He did not come back and I never saw him again. In the opinion of this preacher, religion has nothing at all to do with public affairs. For him, religion begins and ends with modesty for women, moral virtues, and performing religious obligations, so he has no enthusiasm for discussing political rights and public freedoms. He also knows that discussing these subjects in Egypt carries a heavy price and he does not want to pay it.

I referred to religious books to understand Islam's verdict on election rigging and I found that sins are divided into major sins and minor sins. Major sins are those that deserve punishment by God in this life and in the afterlife, and although jurists disagree on details they all agree that bearing false witness is one of the gravest of the major sins. The Qur'an itself strongly advises against bearing false witness in more than one verse; for example, *and those who bear not false witness* (25:72) and *eschew the speaking of falsehood* (22:30). Bearing false witness is lying deliberately in order to undermine justice. When someone stands in front of a judge and testifies falsely, he commits a grave sin because through his false testimony he deprives people of their due and confers it wrongly on those who do not deserve it. In their condemnation of false testimony some jurists go so far as to couple it with idolatry and even say that it cannot be absolved by repentance or by performing the pilgrimage until the offender has made amends to those who lost their rights, or until he at least confesses to them his crime and asks their forgiveness.

Bearing false witness, which Islam considers to be one of the gravest of faults and one of the most horrendous crimes, is the equivalent in contemporary life to rigging elections, no more and no less, because the civil servant who takes part in rigging elections bears false witness to fake results and prevents the winning candidate from obtaining the position that is his or her due while giving the position to someone who does not deserve it. In fact, in my opinion, rigging elections is much worse than bearing false witness, because bearing false witness deprives an individual or a family of their due whereas rigging elections deprives the whole nation of its due. If the fraudsters in the Ministry of Interior realized that from the religious point of view they are bearing false witness they would refuse to take part in the rigging process, but like many Egyptians they consider elections, democracy, and the rotation of power to be secondary matters that have nothing to do with religion. This limited understanding of religion makes us susceptible to despotism and more submissive in the face of injustice, and it explains why despotism is more widespread in Islamic countries than elsewhere.

People progress only in two cases: either when they understand religion properly as primarily the defense of human values—truth, justice, and freedom—or when they start with an ethical concept that makes the human conscience the arbiter that sets the criteria for virtue and honesty. But in countries where religion is understood as detached from human values, talents and resources will go to waste and the people are bound to fall behind in the march of civilization. Limited understanding that ignores the spirit of religion and turns religion into a set of procedures leads mankind to false formal piety and undermines the natural sense of conscience. It may even drive a man to behave appallingly while confident of his own piety, which he thinks is limited to performing religious obligations. The state of affairs in Egypt has sunk to rock bottom, and it is no longer possible to stay silent. Millions of Egyptians live in inhumane conditions, amid poverty, unemployment, disease, repression, and unprecedented corruption. These people have a right to a dignified and humane life. The change we demand will come from the top of the political pyramid and equally from the base. It is our duty to put pressure on the regime until it allows proper elections, but at the same time we have to explain to people that those who take part in rigging elections are committing a grave sin and a despicable crime against their country. When the president gives his orders to rig elections and finds that no police officer or civil servant in the Interior Ministry will agree to soil his honor and his religion by taking part in the rigging, only then will the future begin in Egypt.

Democracy is the solution.

April 19, 2010

Do We Need a Benevolent Dictator?

Last Wednesday was a bad day for Gordon Brown, the British prime minister and leader of the Labour Party. He was making an electoral tour in the northwestern town of Rochdale and while he was talking to people in the street a woman named Gillian Duffy appeared, a retired civil servant sixty-six years old. Ms. Duffy had a heated discussion with Brown in front of the television cameras and she complained about immigrants from Eastern Europe, saying they have taken jobs from British people. The prime minister tried to persuade her that his government's policy on immigration is right, but Duffy stuck to her position. All Brown could do was end the debate gracefully and ask her about her children and grandchildren. He then shook her hand politely and hurried back to his car to catch his next appointment. But unfortunately for Brown he forgot to turn off the small microphone attached to his lapel, and so the microphone continued to broadcast to the television networks what Brown was telling his aides in the car. Brown was angry about his encounter with Duffy and said, "That was a disaster. They should never have put me with that woman. Whose idea was that? . . . She was just a bigoted woman." All the media carried Brown's words and within an hour the gaffe was the talk of Britain. The prime minister had insulted a British citizen, accusing her of bigotry simply because she disagreed with him. When Duffy heard through the media what Brown thought of her, she was most upset, so just a few days before the general elections in Britain on May 6, Brown was in a difficult position. He called Duffy on the phone to apologize but that was not enough. Brown later appeared on British television and the presenter was tough. He played Brown a recording of what he had said about the woman and asked the prime minister if he blamed himself for what happened. Brown said he did blame himself and would never do the same again, and he then made an apology to Duffy in front of the whole country. But even that was not enough to enable the prime minister to put his heinous act behind him. He had to go back to Rochdale and visit Duffy at home, where he spent forty minutes and repeated his apology. Finally Duffy accepted the prime minister's apology but she refused to come outside with him to announce in front of the media that she had forgiven him. So Brown went out alone and announced once again that he had made a mistake and regretted it but now he was relieved that Duffy had graciously accepted his apology.

At the same time that the British prime minister was insisting on apologizing to an ordinary British citizen simply because he described her as bigoted in a private conversation recorded by mistake, hundreds of Egyptians had been sleeping for months on the street in front of the cabinet office and parliament, along with their wives and children. These people were representative of the millions of poor Egyptians whose standard of living has fallen so low that they cannot support their children, but Prime Minister Ahmed Nazif has never taken the trouble to go out and listen to these poor people or to try to help them in any way. On the contrary he abandoned them and went on holiday to Hurghada with his new wife. As for the young people demonstrating in favor of amending the constitution and demanding freedom and an end to the emergency law, they have been beaten up, dragged away, and detained by Central Security Forces (the Egyptian army of occupation), and some members of parliament from the ruling party have even suggested they should be shot.

This vast difference between the behavior of the two prime ministers—one in Egypt and one in Britain—must make us pose the question: Why do the authorities in Britain treat their citizens with such respect while the authorities in Egypt treat people as though they are criminals or animals? The difference here is not ethical; it is political. There's no evidence that Gordon Brown is more moral than Ahmed Nazif, but Brown is an elected prime minister in a democratic system, so he knows that he is the servant of the people, who are the source of all power. He also knows that if he lost the trust of the voters then his political life would be over. Ahmed Nazif, on the other hand, is not elected in the first place but appointed by President Mubarak, so what matters to him is not people's confidence but the approval of the president. Similarly, no one elected

President Mubarak, who seized power thirty years ago through repression and rigged elections, so it does not matter much to him whether Egyptians have confidence in him as long as he can subjugate them through the security agencies. If Gordon Brown ruled Britain by fraud and by emergency law, he would not have apologized to Gillian Duffy. In fact he would probably have had her arrested and sent to the nearest State Security office, where she would have been beaten, strung up by her legs, and electrocuted in sensitive parts of her body. Maybe Duffy would be tried in a State Security emergency court on charges of causing trouble, insulting a symbol of the state, and endangering social peace in Britain.

It's the way the ruler has obtained power that determines his behavior while in power. This fact, which is well established in the developed world, still escapes some Egyptians, who judge a ruler on his policies in office and do not pay much attention to how he came to power. Some Egyptians still dream of a benevolent dictator who would be above all laws but would use his overwhelming power to ensure justice. The concept of the benevolent dictator, just like the concepts of the noble thief or the honest whore, is no more than a meaningless fantasy. How can a dictator be benevolent when dictatorship in itself is patently unjust? But the concept has infiltrated Arab thinking over many centuries of despotism. It would be fair to mention here that genuine Islam offered a great democratic model many centuries before Europe did. The Prophet Muhammad did not choose a successor because he wanted Muslims to be free to choose their ruler. In fact, three of the first four caliphs were chosen by the people and remained accountable to the people, as happens today in the best democratic systems. As soon as Abu Bakr, the first ruler in Islam, took office, he said in a sermon, "I have been given the authority over you, and I am not the best of you. If I do well, help me; and if I do wrong, set me right. . . . Obey me so long as I obey God and His Messenger. But if I disobey God and His Messenger, you owe me no obedience."

This great sermon predates modern constitutions by centuries in defining the democratic relationship between the ruler and the ruled, but the democracy of early Islam quickly disappeared and long centuries of despotism followed, with the sultan's jurists putting religion at the service of the ruler, stripping Muslims of their political rights and laying the foundations for two very bad and dangerous ideas. The first idea is that power belongs to the winner, which gives legitimacy to all those who usurp power as long as they can hold on to it by force. The second idea is that Muslims have a duty to obey the ruler even if he is oppressive and corrupt. These ideas have created a gap in Muslims' awareness of democracy, making them prone to be submissive and more tolerant of despotism than other peoples. Conditions in Egypt have reached rock bottom and most Egyptians have started calling for the kind of change that will bring them justice, dignity, and freedom. We have to understand that change will never come about through one person, however noble his intentions or faultless his morals. Change will come about through a just new system that treats Egyptians as fully competent citizens with full rights, not as subjects or slaves who exist to please the ruler. When Egyptians are able, by their own free will, to choose who governs and who represents them in parliament, when Egyptians are all equal before the law, only then will the future begin and the president in Egypt will be as concerned with the dignity of every citizen as demonstrated in Britain last week.

Democracy is the solution.

May 3, 2010

A Story for Children and Adults

The old elephant was under the big tree on the riverbank, the place where he usually met his assistants, but this time he could not stand on his own four legs, so he knelt down and his trunk rested on the ground beside him. He looked so completely exhausted that it was a major effort for him to keep his eyes open and follow what was happening around him. Next to him stood his four assistants, the donkey, the pig, the wolf, and the fox, which seemed tense and started the conversation, saying, "Brothers, our great forest is going through trying and difficult times. Our lord the old elephant is still suffering the effects of his recent disease and I have heard that all the animals in the forest are coming this way in a protest march led by the giraffe."

The donkey brayed loudly and said, "Why does this giraffe insist on causing trouble?"

The pig, whose body gave off a foul smell, squealed to object. "I suggest we kill this giraffe to be rid of him," he said.

The fox looked at the donkey and the pig with disdain and said, "Really, I've never seen anyone as stupid as you two. The problem is not with the giraffe. All the animals are disgruntled and we have to negotiate with them and reach some compromise."

The wolf howled and said, "I'm sorry, fox. . . . We won't negotiate with anyone. The king of the jungle, the old elephant, is still alive, God preserve him, and his son, the young elephant, Daghfal, will succeed him on the throne."

The fox smiled and said, "Let's be frank. Daghfal isn't fit to rule. He plays all the time and isn't responsible. Look what he's doing now."

They all looked over at the young elephant and found him rolling happily in the grass, flapping his vast ears, sucking water up his trunk and then spraying it on his body. He did indeed seem to be too fun-loving and carefree for the difficult times the jungle was going through.

The fox continued: "All I ask of you is that you keep quiet and leave me to come to terms with the angry animals."

At this point the wolf snarled and said, "Since when did we have to take those wretched animals into account? We decide what we want and they just obey our orders."

The fox smiled and said, "You would be wise to realize that the situation in the jungle has changed. The animals today are not as they were yesterday. Being tough won't work any longer."

"On the contrary. Now we need to be tougher than ever. We own everything. We have a trained army of dogs fierce enough to subdue any animal that lifts its head against us."

The fox was about to speak when suddenly the sound of all the animals together rang through the jungle. A mixture of all the species—rabbits, chickens, cows, buffalo, sheep, cats, and monkeys, and even fairground monkeys—joined the march. They advanced from all over the forest, with the elegant giraffe striding at their head. They came close to where the old elephant was lying. Suddenly the wolf shouted out, "Who are you and what do you want?"

The giraffe shouted back, "We are the inhabitants of this jungle and we have grievances we want to submit to the elephant king."

"This isn't the time for grievances. The king is tired and busy. Go away."

The giraffe swung his long neck right and left. "We won't go away until we've submitted our grievances."

"How dare you be so bold!"

The fox intervened and said, "Okay, calm down, giraffe. What are these grievances?"

The giraffe replied, "This jungle belongs to all of us but we see none of the benefits. You rule the jungle in your own interests and don't care about the other animals. All of the benefits go to the donkey, the pig, the wolf, and the fox. The other animals do an honest day's work but still don't have enough food for their children."

The wolf was about to speak but the giraffe continued with gusto: "The situation in the jungle has hit rock bottom in every way. You have indigestion from eating too much while we die of hunger. We can't take it any longer."

The rebellious animals cheered at length in support of the giraffe, their leader. The wolf stuck his head out and shouted, "Go away. I don't want to hear what you say. Off you go!"

"We won't go." It was the giraffe who spoke and it seemed clear that he would not back down. At that point the wolf looked up and gave a long howl, and instantly dozens of trained dogs appeared and started to growl defiantly at the animals. In the past the sight of these dogs had been enough to strike terror into the hearts of the jungle inhabitants, but this time they stood their ground against the dogs. Amazed, the donkey said, "They're not afraid of the guard dogs. My God! What's happened to our jungle?"

The giraffe said, "Wolf, you and your colleagues have to understand that we're no longer afraid of you. We're no longer afraid of anything, even death. Either you give us our rights or we'll have to fight you."

The guard dogs advanced in combat formation in a semicircle, ready to attack. They opened their mouths, showed their sharp teeth, and started to snarl. The sight was truly frightening but the giraffe did not flinch. "You're in a strange position, you guard dogs," said the giraffe. "You're fighting us on behalf of the elephant and his assistants, although you really belong on our side, not on theirs. Just like us, you are victims of injustice and poverty. We've all lost the same rights. Why are you supporting the despotic elephant against us? He's using you and when he no longer needs you he'll throw you by the wayside."

Some of the dogs seemed to hesitate. The giraffe went on the attack and all the animals attacked behind him. The dogs grappled with them savagely. Much blood was spilled and many dead fell on both sides. The strange thing is that many of the dogs were moved by what the giraffe had said and did not take part in the fighting, which enabled the animals to triumph over the other guard dogs. When the fox realized that defeat was certain he ran off, leaving no trace behind him. The wolf crouched on the ground, then made a single pounce at the giraffe, digging his powerful teeth into its chest. But despite the severe pain and the copious bleeding, the giraffe climbed to its feet, thought hard, and then aimed a firm kick at the wolf's head, crushing its skull instantly. The donkey and the pig were so stupid that they were unable to act until the animals mobbed them and finished them off. Then the animals found themselves face to face with the elephant king and his son, Daghfal.

The giraffe went up to them and said, "Old elephant, your reign has come to an end today. I still remember how the animals had high hopes at the beginning of your reign, but you surrounded yourself with the worst and dirtiest animals and now you can see the result for yourself."

In a tired voice, the old elephant replied, "I've always done what I thought was right. If I made any mistakes then forgive me."

"We'll treat you with respect," the giraffe said, "because you were once a good elephant. We'll let you leave peacefully with your son, the young elephant, Daghfal. Go now and never come back to this forest. We've suffered enough from your corrupt and oppressive governance."

The old elephant nodded his head, lifted his trunk slowly and with difficulty, and looked almost grateful.

The giraffe turned to the animals and cried, "The reign of tyranny is over, never to return!"

The animals all cheered, declaring with enthusiasm their joy at freedom.

Democracy is the solution.

May 25, 2010

A Surprise Dinner with
an Important Person

One of my friends invited me to dinner at a well-known restaurant on a boat on the Nile. My friend and I sat down at the table reserved for us and the waiter rushed up to greet us and ask us if we wanted a drink before eating. My friend ordered a lemon juice, while I asked for a cold bottle of nonalcoholic beer. We chatted a while, then my friend looked surprised. He leaned over to me and whispered, "Well, I never! Do you know who that is?"

"Who?"

"It's Gamal Mubarak."

I looked around slowly to see him. My friend noticed how excited I was at this coincidence and said, "Would you like to sit where I am so you can see better?"

The offer was tempting. I sat in his place and saw Gamal Mubarak, the president's son, sitting with his wife, Khadiga. He was wearing a dark-blue blazer and a white shirt without a tie while his wife was wearing an elegant blue dress. I was surprised not to see any bodyguards around them. I couldn't see what Khadiga was eating but Gamal Mubarak was eating with relish a pizza napoletana. I watched them for several minutes and then something unexpected happened. Gamal Mubarak looked at me and smiled, greeted me with a nod, and then beckoned me to approach. I took leave of my friend and was heading toward his table when a burly, fierce-looking man suddenly blocked my way with his body. I caught a glimpse of a large pistol in a holster under his jacket. Gamal Mubarak said something to him I didn't catch and the man backed off to let me pass.

Gamal Mubarak smiled and said, "Good to meet you."

"Good to meet you, too."

"By the way, Khadiga and I are among your readers."

"It's an honor."

The waiter came and I ordered half a grilled chicken, fries, and another cold bottle of nonalcoholic beer. I asked Gamal Mubarak after his father's health and he answered quietly, "Well enough."

After that we spoke about the food and all three of us said how much we admired the proficiency of the Lebanese restaurant owner. I was fighting an urge to speak out and in the end I could not resist. "Mr. Mubarak," I said, "I thank you for your hospitality and your generosity, but there's something I have to say and I fear it might spoil the pleasure of the occasion."

"Feel free to speak your mind," he said.

"Things in Egypt are very bad. We've hit rock bottom," I said.

He looked at me with interest and said, "It's true we have big problems, but this is the price we have to pay for development."

"Where's this development?"

"In the last few years the government has achieved unprecedented rates of growth."

"With all due respect, where's the development you talk about when half of all Egyptians live below the poverty line? Haven't you heard about the young men who kill themselves because of poverty and unemployment?" I asked.

"We in the policies committee of the National Democratic Party have detailed studies on all these problems," he said.

"Mr. Mubarak, most of what the people close to you in the policies committee keep telling you isn't true. They're opportunists and they're pushing you as successor to your father for the sake of their personal interests," I said.

"What do you mean by 'successor'?"

"I mean you inheriting the presidency from President Mubarak," I said.

"Don't I have the right to take part in politics, like any citizen? If I ran for the presidency and won the elections, would that be 'inheritance'?" he asked.

"You well know that elections in Egypt are a formality and are rigged. Would you be proud if you won the presidency by repression and fraud?"

"No elections anywhere in the world are without irregularities, and

I think you're exaggerating on this question of repression," said Mr. Mubarak.

"Mr. Mubarak, are you living in the same country as us? There's a difference between irregularities and the organized vote rigging that takes place in Egypt. As for repression, you only have to go on the Internet to see sad stories about the detentions, torture, and repression Egyptians are subjected to. Have you heard about Khaled Said, who was killed by the police in Alexandria?" I asked.

Khadiga spoke up, saying, "I felt very sorry for that young man."

"I made a statement demanding that justice take its course," said Mr. Mubarak.

"What use is that? What's needed is a repeal of the emergency law under which thousands of Egyptians are tortured," I said.

Gamal Mubarak put his knife and fork down next to his plate and took a gulp of the orange juice in front of him. Then suddenly, in a loud voice, he said, "It's easy to talk but it's hard to act. Your job is writing stories and articles, whereas I've been working twelve hours a day for years to reform the country."

I was annoyed at the change in his tone but decided to go on to the end. "First, writing is a very hard job," I said. "Second, even if you've worked hard, what matters is the results of your efforts. Listen, Mr. Mubarak, in what capacity do you work?"

"I'm the chairman of the policies committee in the National Democratic Party," he replied.

"Would you have obtained that position if you weren't the president's son?"

He looked at me with obvious anger and for the first time I felt he regretted inviting me to his table. Khadiga smiled and looked at her husband to try to calm him down, but in a loud voice he said, "Of course you have the right to think we haven't achieved anything in the policies committee, but many people appreciate what we've done, thank God, in Egypt and abroad."

"Where's this appreciation you're talking about? The editors of the government newspapers praise you because they depend on you for favors. The poor people who come out to greet you on your tours are recruited by the party and the security agencies. But in the international press there are serious criticisms of the idea of hereditary succession. Did you read what Joseph Mayton wrote in *The Guardian* last year?"

"Yes, I did."

"What did he write?" asked Khadiga.

Gamal Mubarak turned to her and said, "Joseph Mayton wrote that I represent everything that's wrong with Egypt. Okay, that's his opinion, but there are many different opinions. Many international newspapers write fair things about me."

"I'm sorry to say it but the papers that are most friendly toward you are the Israeli papers. Haven't you thought about the reason for that? The lengthy tribute which *Maariv* wrote this week is worth thinking about," I said.

"What do you mean?" he asked.

"Do you think Israel wishes Egypt well?"

"Of course not," Khadiga chipped in.

Gamal Mubarak thought a little, then said, "And if we suppose that Israel's intentions are always bad, what do you mean to say?"

"This Israeli insistence on seeing you succeed to the presidency reflects the Israelis' alarm at the idea of Egypt turning democratic. They well understand that Egypt has the potential to be a great nation and that if it became democratic it would rise in the world and take the Arab world up with it. So they defend the idea of succession so that Egypt remains as wretched as possible."

Gamal Mubarak sighed and was about to stand up. "Anyway, it was good to meet you," he said.

"Before you go, I have another question," I said.

"Please make it quick."

"Do you love Egypt, Mr. Mubarak?"

"Of course."

"Loving Egypt means its interests must take precedence over your own. I want you to promise me now that you'll finally abandon the idea of hereditary succession and work with Egyptians for democratic reform," I said.

Gamal Mubarak looked at me and his lips began to move but his voice was suddenly interrupted. I heard a persistent ringing noise and a dazzling light filled the room. I opened my eyes with difficulty and found my wife in front of me holding a jar of honey, as usual when she wakes me in the morning. She smiled and said, "Good morning."

"Good morning."

"Who's this Gamal you were talking about in your sleep?" she asked.

"Gamal Mubarak. You see, we made an agreement to support democracy."

"Gamal Mubarak support democracy just like that?" she said. "Okay, open your mouth."

I opened my mouth and took a large spoonful of honey.

Democracy is the solution.

July 20, 2010

Thoughts on the President's Health

I n the 1980s I was studying in the United States for a master's degree in dentistry and at the same time interning as a doctor in the University of Illinois hospital in Chicago. The patients who came to the hospital were poor Americans, most of them black. Every patient had an accurate medical file that contained his or her medical history, the details of his or her health, and test results. The first thing we learned as doctors was that the medical file was confidential and no one could look at it without the permission of the patient. In other words, people's medical details were treated as personal secrets protected by law in the United States. During that period it happened that Ronald Reagan, who was president at the time, had an unexpected health crisis, was taken to hospital, and had surgery to remove a polyp from his intestines. From the first day there were official statements on all the details of his ailment, the type of surgery he had, and its possible side effects. In fact U.S. television networks invited a group of doctors and asked them all about the effects that the medicines Reagan was taking would have on his powers of concentration and his psychological condition. I was amazed when the doctors asserted that these medicines would make him unfit to take decisions for three weeks, after which he would return to normal.

The truth is, I saw quite a contrast there. Poor and simple U.S. citizens who came to the university hospital had medical files no one could look at without their permission, but when the president fell ill the American people had a right to know everything about his ailment and the drugs he was taking. The idea here is one of the basic principles of a democratic system. An ordinary citizen does not have a public position so his health is something that concerns him alone and his private life is protected by law, whereas the president is a public servant elected by citizens to perform a certain role for a fixed term, and in some cases he loses his job immediately if they withdraw their confidence. In a democratic system the president is the servant of the people in the full sense of the word and as soon as he takes office he loses his privacy and his whole life is exposed to the world. The public has the right to know the most intricate details of his life, from the source and size of his wealth, to his romantic ties, to even his health and the diseases he has, because the decisions the president takes affect the lives of millions of people and if he makes a bad judgment or is psychologically disturbed, it could lead to a disaster for which the country and citizens would all pay the price.

I remembered all this when I was following the current furor in Egypt over the health of President Mubarak. Several international newspapers have published reports claiming that President Mubarak's health is deteriorating. In response to these reports President Mubarak has made several public appearances and the government has launched a countercampaign in which officials have denied that the president is ill and have said that he is in the best of health. They have even said that the civil servants who work with President Mubarak, who is eighty-two, run after him panting and have trouble keeping up with him because of his extraordinary dynamism and vigor. But western newspaper reports on President Mubarak's illness did not stop, but rather increased. At that point orders went out to the chief editors of government newspapers, who then started a full-scale press campaign asserting that the president is in excellent health and strongly condemning the western press reports, which they saw as decisive proof of a major Zionist-imperialist conspiracy designed to undermine Egyptians' confidence in their president's health. Of course, we wish the president good health and a long life (as we do for everyone), but this does raise a question: Instead of these press campaigns and accusations of a conspiracy by international newspapers, why doesn't the government resort to objective methods to make statements about President Mubarak's health in a convincing manner?

The difference between what happened when the U.S. president was ill and what happened with the Egyptian president's illness is exactly the difference between a democratic system and despotic rule. In a democratic system the president is seen as an ordinary person who can fall ill like the rest of humanity without appearing weak or losing prestige. But in despotic regimes the head of state is not portrayed as an ordinary human but as an inspired and unique leader of unequalled wisdom and courage, in fact as a legend rarely matched in the history of the nation. So disease, with all the pain, suffering, and human weakness it evokes, is incompatible with the image of the legendary president as someone above ordinary humans. In a democratic system a presidential illness might cause concern for the future of the president but not for the future of the country. If the president in a democratic system retires, the system allows citizens to choose his successor easily and simply. But in a despotic regime the future of the country and its citizens is in the hands of the president alone, so his illness poses a real danger to the coherence and well-being of the country. If an autocratic president is driven out of power by disease, the whole country starts on a voyage into the unknown and no one knows how long it will last or how it will end.

Another important difference is that a democratic president always feels that he owes his position to the people who chose him in free elections and that those who brought him to office have a right to know about his health, in order to be sure that he can perform his duties properly. But in Egypt the president comes to power through referendums and elections that are a mere formality, and holds on to power by force, so he does not feel that he owes his position to the people. On the contrary, sycophantic writers and officials often say that the president has done Egyptians a great favor by sacrificing his comfort for their sake and so Egyptians should do their best to prove they are worthy of their great president.

In this topsy-turvy state of affairs Egyptians do not have the right to know more about the president than he wants to disclose, in whatever way His Excellency sees fit for the people. The president only has to say he is well and we should thank God and shut up, not a single word after that. Officials see asking persistent questions about the president's health as licentious conduct indicative of impertinence and bad breeding, and possibly a sign of treason and of ties to some foreign and hostile sponsor. Under similar circumstances two years ago, journalist Ibrahim Eissa wrote several articles asking questions about rumors that the president was ill. These articles were seen as a crime against the country, and Ibrahim Eissa stood trial and was sentenced to prison, only to be saved from that fate by a presidential pardon. The message was clear: beware of saying more than you should about the president's illness because the president might get angry, and if the president gets angry with you then a black fate awaits you. Only a presidential pardon can save you from the president's wrath, because in Egypt the president's will is above the law, or rather it is in fact the law.

The way the regime handled the international press reports on the health of President Mubarak reveals the real crisis in the concept of government in Egypt, because yet again the regime has proved that it does not see Egyptians as citizens but as subjects who have never had the right to choose their rulers freely and so do not have the right to know whether President Mubarak is ill or if he intends to stay in office or retire or even what will happen if the president leaves office for any reason. In the eyes of the despotic regime, the Egyptian people do not deserve to choose, to ask, or to know. This distorted concept of government does not stem from the nature of the ruler as much as from the nature of the system. The way he came to office imposes on the ruler a certain vision and behavior while he is in office. When and only when Egyptians win back their natural right to choose their rulers, the ruler will change from being a unique legend into being merely a public servant to the people, and Egyptians will have the right to precise and lucid information about his health. That's when Egypt will rise and start its future.

Democracy is the solution.

August 3, 2010

Why Don't Egyptians Take Part in Elections?

When Egyptians rose up in 1919 against the British occupation, and nationalist leader Saad Zaghloul went to Paris to submit the demands of the Egyptian nation to the peace conference that followed the First World War, the British government reacted with a skillful maneuver: sending a fact-finding committee to Egypt under Colonial Secretary Lord Milner. But Egyptians quickly saw through the trick and realized that to have any dealings with the Milner Commission would undermine the credibility of Saad Zaghloul as a leader with a mandate from the Egyptian people. When the commission arrived in Cairo, it found a complete boycott awaiting it. Not a single Egyptian politician agreed to cooperate with the commission and the prime minister of the time, Mohamed Said Pasha, had to resign to avoid having to deal with Lord Milner. The lord is said to have lost his way in the streets of Cairo one day and when his driver asked a passerby for directions, the man replied, "Tell your Englishman to ask Saad Zaghloul Pasha in Paris." As a result of this national consensus, the Milner Commission failed in its task and the British government had to bow to the will of Egyptians and negotiate directly with Saad Zaghloul.

You will find this intense political consciousness among the Egyptian people on every page of Egypt's history, without exception. The intellectuals and politicians analyze everything based on theories and preconceived ideas, talk much, and take part in complex debates in which they always disagree, whereas ordinary people, even if they are less well educated, often have a sound political instinct that gives them shrewd insight into everything that happens, and they adopt the correct position with amazing ease. Forty years after the death of President Gamal Abdel Nasser, we are still debating his mistakes and his achievements, whereas the Egyptian people gave their opinion when Abdel Nasser died and millions of Egyptians came out to attend his funeral. These simple people who sobbed like children in mourning for Abdel Nasser were well aware of all his mistakes and knew that he was responsible for a cruel defeat for Egypt and the Arab nation, but they also understood that he was a great leader with a rare commitment to his principles and that he had done his best and devoted his life to his country. When we intellectuals face a confusion of choices we must always listen to the people. Ordinary Egyptians are by no means rabble or riffraff who do not know their own best interests, as Egyptian officials say. On the contrary, they usually have an infallible compass by which they determine the correct political position. Many intellectuals may stray from the nationalist path and become accessories and propagandists for the despotic regime, and we should bear in mind that intellectuals who lose their way always start by despising the people. We can understand our country only if we understand the people, and we cannot understand the people unless we respect their abilities and their way of thinking, listen to their opinions and experiences, and deal with them not as creatures of deficient intelligence and competence who need us as mentors but as people who have experience of life and from whom we should learn.

In a few weeks parliamentary elections will begin and the regime has refused to provide any guarantees that the elections will be fair. It has refused to repeal the emergency law or to purge the electoral registers of the names of dead people (who always vote for the ruling party), and it has rejected judicial supervision and even international monitoring. All the indications confirm that the next elections will be rigged, like all previous elections. In such circumstances Egyptians decide to boycott elections and despite the regime's desperate efforts the turnout is never more than 10 percent of the electorate. The question here is: Why don't Egyptians go to the polls? In fact, when Egyptians boycott elections, it is not at all a sign of passivity, as the regime's propagandists repeatedly say. It is a conscious decision, effective and sound. If the elections are rigged and it is impossible to prevent electoral fraud, then boycotting them is the right choice, because it prevents the regime from claiming that it represents the people it rules. That's why the regime is so vociferous in urging Egyptians to take part in the coming elections. The scenario has been written and produced and all the roles have been assigned. All they need is a cast of extras for the show to begin. The Egyptian people are not at all passive; they have grown wise from experience accumulated over many centuries.

The evidence for this is that Egyptians are keen to take part in any credible elections. Last year I went to vote in the elections at the sports club I belong to and found crowds of club members who had come on their day off to stand in long lines to elect new board members. I had an idea and started asking the club members if they voted in parliamentary or presidential elections. Most of those I asked looked at me with scorn and said they never took part in government elections because they are rigged, and some of them said they were not registered to vote in the first place. The truth is as clear as the sun in Egypt: a despotic and oppressive regime, which has failed and which has monopolized power for thirty years by means of repression and fraud until Egypt has hit rock bottom in all spheres of life, is asking people to take part in rigged elections in order to obtain fraudulent and superficial legitimacy. So boycotting the coming elections is the proper position. Simple Egyptians will boycott the elections because they do not want official posts; they do not dream of becoming members of parliament, they do not have investments they are frightened of losing, and they do not have friendly relations with the security agencies.

Some weeks ago we were reading in the newspapers about debates in the political parties over whether to boycott the elections or take part. The question to ask here is: Is there a single guarantee that real elections will take place? Has the regime given any commitment not to rig them and, even if it did, has this regime ever met any of its commitments? What's the point of any party going into elections when it knows in advance they will be rigged? They say they will take part in the elections in order to put the government to shame, but hasn't the government been shamed enough times already? Besides, what are these parties and what have they done in recent decades for the millions of poor people? What have the parties done to prevent torture, repression, and corruption? The answer is zilch, nothing. Most of these parties are paper puppets on strings held by the regime. Some of the party leaders cooperate with the security agencies and some of them are such favorites of the regime (which they claim to oppose) that they are appointed members of the upper house of parliament. So their position is worthless if they take part in rigged elections in return for one or two seats in a parliament that has lost legitimacy.

It would be truly regrettable if the Muslim Brotherhood were implicated in taking part in rigged elections. It seems that the Brotherhood is destined never to learn from its mistakes. Anyone who reads the history of the Brotherhood will be amazed at the vast difference between its nationalist positions against foreign occupation and its attitudes toward despotism. The Brotherhood played an honorable and important role in the Palestine war of 1948, led the Egyptian resistance against the British in the Suez Canal towns in 1951, and set a fine example of sacrifice and courage. But, sadly, in most of its positions on domestic matters the Brotherhood has put the organization's interests before the interests of the nation and has invariably stood on the side of despotism. It supported King Farouk and Prime Minister Ismail Sidki, the butcher of the people. It backed Abdel Nasser when he abolished parliamentary life. It supported President Anwar Sadat and overlooked his repressive measures. When it comes to the possibility of President Hosni Mubarak passing the presidency to his son, Gamal, some Muslim Brothers have made vague and ambiguous statements that can be read in conflicting ways. If the Brotherhood does take part in the coming elections, it will be giving this iniquitous regime a fraudulent legitimacy it desperately needs and will play the role of the wretched extra in a drama for which all Egyptians will pay the price.

Those who advocate for taking part in the elections fall into three groups: they are either simpletons who do not understand what is happening around them, people seeking office at any price, or stooges who receive their instructions from the regime and have to carry them out. Boycotting the coming elections is the correct position, which the Egyptian people will adopt, and so anyone who does take part will be acting in defiance of the will of the nation. When Egypt has real elections we will all take part, but for now, let's leave them to act out their silly and boring drama alone, without extras.

Democracy is the solution.

September 9, 2010

THE PEOPLE AND
SOCIAL JUSTICE

Our Advice to the Butcher

My family used to have an empty apartment in Mawardi Street in Sayyida Zeinab and I used to stay there to be alone while studying for exams at university. In that apartment I saw extraordinary vignettes of working-class Egyptian life.

Opposite us, on the second floor of a dilapidated old building, lived a butcher by the name of Mr. Galal, a stocky man with a fierce temper. He was fond of alcohol and every night he would drink the cheapest and deadliest varieties available. When he was drunk, he turned into a raging bull and as soon as he arrived home toward dawn everyone in the street would wake up to the screams of his wife calling out for help as he beat her mercilessly. Some of the residents, including me, sympathized with the poor woman and we would stand on the pavement opposite where we could see Mr. Galal's room, shouting out good advice: "Don't let the devil tempt you, Mr. Galal!" "It's best to make peace, folks."

The leader in these mediation attempts was "Uncle" Awad, the grain merchant, a thin man of more than seventy who was also a man of considerable wisdom and courage. One night Galal the butcher was arguing as usual with his wife, but this time the argument escalated and suddenly we saw him bring out a large knife. The sight of it glinting alarmed us as we stood on the pavement opposite, watching and trying to calm the man down. His wife's cries broke the silence of the night: "Save me, people. He's going to kill me." Mr. Galal growled back, "I'll finish you off. Say your last prayers."

At this point Awad the grain merchant, with us behind him, rushed upstairs to the butcher's apartment and began to pound on the door with such violence and insistence that in the end Mr. Galal had to come and open the door for us. We rushed inside, pulled the woman away from him, formed a circle around him with our bodies, and grabbed the knife from him. We started to calm him down and did not leave until we had reconciled the couple.

The next day the butcher came to "Uncle" Awad to complain. "Do you think it's right to come between a man and his wife?" he asked.

"Of course it is, if he's going to kill her," Awad replied at once.

"Even if I kill her, she's my wife and I can do what I like with her."

"Of course not. How can you kill her and say you can do what you like?"

"I don't allow anyone to interfere in my household."

At that point Awad looked at the butcher long and hard, then calmly said, "If you don't want anyone interfering in your household then you should show some self-respect."

I remembered this incident while I was following the case of Ayman Nour, the politician who challenged President Mubarak in the 2005 elections. I don't know the man personally, and I disagree with him on many things, but I defend his rights as a citizen. The government allowed him to set up the Ghad Party, but as soon as the party began its political activity by calling for constitutional amendments and presidential elections with more than one candidate, the government turned on it. Ayman Nour's parliamentary immunity was lifted in ten minutes, he was detained, beaten, and humiliated, his wife was threatened with prosecution on trumped-up immorality charges if she defended him, and the government newspapers suddenly discovered that Ayman Nour was the worst person in Egypt and in the Arab world, guilty of every possible vice. The sycophantic scribes said that even his doctorate was a worthless fake. What was behind this volte-face? The government said it was prosecuting Ayman Nour because he submitted forged signatures when he applied to set up his political party, but this is an accusation that would not convince a young child. The head of a political party is not such a forensic expert that he can tell with his naked eye if the stamps on the documents are forged or genuine. Besides, by law a party needs fifty signatures to submit an application for official recognition, while Ayman Nour had collected five thousand signatures, so he had no need for forged signatures in the first place. It's clear that the security agencies slipped in some forged signatures so they could use them to punish Ayman Nour if and when necessary. So the case against him is political, trumped up, and unjust, and it cannot be defended as legitimate. Naturally the western press treated the case as an example of how the Egyptian regime cracks down on its political opponents, at which point Egyptian officials made a great hue and cry, saying they categorically reject foreign interference. I have a few observations to make:

First, any Egyptian patriot opposes foreign interference in the country's affairs for whatever reason, but it is truly surprising that the Egyptian regime objects to foreign interference only when it's about repression against Egyptians. In all other fields the regime welcomes and seeks out foreign interference. In economics and foreign policy the Egyptian regime carries out U.S. instructions to the letter. In fact senior officials have expressed more than once their sympathy for the U.S. Army as it faces growing casualties in Iraq, and have publicly proffered suggestions on how to reduce the casualties. The Egyptian government has said it would be willing to train Iraqi policemen, to strike at the Iraqi resistance, of course, and where was its national pride then? Egypt has met every impertinent U.S. request without objection, from the release of Israeli spy Azam Azam, to sending the Egyptian ambassador back to Israel, to signing the QIZ trade agreement with Israel and the United States. So officials in Egypt have no misgivings about foreign interference in their affairs; in fact they seek it out, they boast of the special relationship with the United States, and, whenever someone tells them Egypt should have an independent national will, they accuse them of inflexible thinking and of being relics of the "totalitarian era." But when the foreign intervention is about repression, detentions, torture, and the other crimes committed against Egyptians, only then do Egyptian officials say foreign interference is unacceptable and brag about national dignity.

Second, the United States is in fact the country least qualified to talk about democracy and human rights. The U.S. Army's crimes at Guantánamo Bay and Abu Ghraib are still fresh in the memory, and since the Second World War, successive U.S. administrations have consistently, in order to protect U.S. interests, provided support to the worst and most despotic Arab rulers. The U.S. record is even dirtier in Latin America, where, by the admission of its own officials, the CIA conspired to overthrow a democratically elected government in Chile in 1973, to kill Chilean President Salvador Allende, and to hand power to U.S. proxies. All this well-known history prevents us from trusting the United States when it talks about democracy. In fairness we should remember that the

West is not just the United States and the imperial powers. There are hundreds of western NGOs, and the volunteers in these NGOs defend human rights as an ideal and expose rights violations everywhere, even in western countries. These organizations are respected, have a voice in the West, and have influence over public opinion there, more so than the governments do. Besides, as a matter of principle and of law, detaining and torturing innocent people cannot be considered part of a country's internal affairs, because these crimes are against humanity as a whole and anyone has the right to condemn them. When the Egyptian regime detains three thousand people in al-Arish in Sinai for months on end without trial, tortures them, gives them electric shocks, and rapes women in front of their husbands and children, these heinous crimes cannot be considered an internal Egyptian affair, because torturing the innocent and violating their humanity is in no way a national matter.

Finally, I hope Egyptian officials realize that the state of affairs is intolerable and cannot continue. President Mubarak, after a quarter of a century in power, is preparing to organize a new referendum in which he will win 99 percent of the votes as usual so that he can stay in power forever, to be succeeded in office by his son, Gamal, and maybe Gamal Mubarak's son after him. We have so much poverty, unemployment, rampant social injustice, repression, vote rigging, and abuse of innocents that life has become impossible for millions of Egyptians.

Important signs of change have appeared recently, and I hope officials understand them before it is too late. I hope they ask themselves: What is it that drove a well-known writer like Mohamed al-Sayed Said to confront the head of state with the truth about the grievous state of the country? How did the Kefaya movement come about and how was it able, in the space of a few months, to persuade thousands of patriotic intellectuals to join? What is it that drove university professors and respected citizens to go out in the streets and face the possibility of being beaten by an army of riot police simply in order to speak out and say "enough" to rule by Mubarak? Why did thousands of students from Cairo University assemble and force open the university gates so they could join the Kefaya movement's latest protest? All of these are sure and unmistakable signs that change is necessary and a price the regime will soon have to pay, whether it likes it or not. Egyptians have a yearning for freedom, justice, and a dignified life. This is the issue. To those who think they have a right to repress Egyptians, like Galal the butcher with his wife, we say, just as

Awad the wise grain merchant said, "If you don't want anyone interfering in your household, then you should show some self-respect."

Words to ponder:

On January 24, Major Mohamed Farid, the head of criminal investigations at Mashtoul al-Souk police station in Sharqiya Province, tortured Mohamed Salem to force him to confess to a theft. This torture resulted in a fracture in Salem's spinal column, which completely paralyzed both legs, made Salem an invalid, and led to fecal and urinary incontinence. (The Egyptian Association against Torture)

State Security headquarters in al-Arish smelled of roasting skin because of the hundreds of detainees being tortured with electric shocks. (*Al-Ahali* newspaper)

Human rights in Egypt have recently seen a significant transformation. (Egyptian Foreign Ministry statement)

We assure you that Ayman Nour was absolutely not beaten. The injury under his left eye came about when his face collided with the finger of one of the policemen as he was being arrested. (People's Assembly statement)

Imagine, God forbid, what would have happened if someone less wise than President Mubarak were ruling Egypt. . . . It would have been a disaster. (Mustafa al-Fiki)

Citizens must be informed in advance before the water is cut off. (President Hosni Mubarak)

February 27, 2005

The Party of the Great Collapse

The official media blackout, statements from the Ministry of Interior, articles by the government's scribes, none of them can diminish the gravity of what happened in central Cairo during the Eid holiday. More than a thousand young men gathered between Adli Street and Talaat Harb Street and started attacking and molesting women at random for four full hours. Any female who had the misfortune to be passing through the area at that time—girls, women, young and old, with or without *hijab* or *niqab*, walking alone, with friends, or even with their husbands—would have met the same fate. Hundreds of sex-crazed young men would have attacked her and completely surrounded her with their bodies, and dozens of hands would have reached out to pull off her clothes and grope her breasts and between her legs. Some people rallied round and saved one or two girls whose clothes had been torn and who were lying in the street half naked.

The girls who were assaulted were not prostitutes or delinquents, just ordinary Egyptians like my wife or your wife, my daughter or your daughter, whose only crime was to believe that we live in a decent country and to have gone out for a walk at the Eid holiday. This heinous crime took place in front of dozens of witnesses. Many photographers took pictures of it and posted their pictures on the Internet. I have seen the pictures and I grieved for my country. I will never forget the girl in the *hijab* who appeared in the pictures with her clothes completely shredded (though the fiends forgot to tear off her head covering) as dozens of hands groped her naked body. I will never forget the sorrowful and pained expression on her face as she was violated in the street. She resisted the assault as much as she could but in the end she collapsed.

What happened is not just a crime but also a moral and social catastrophe we need to analyze in order to understand what is happening in Egypt. First, the young men involved come from poor unplanned districts of the city, from the lowest strata of Egyptian society. Initially they gathered to buy movie tickets, but when they discovered the tickets were sold out they went on an angry rampage, smashing the facade of the Metro movie theater. When they realized there were no police in the whole area and felt that their numbers gave them strength and made them immune to punishment, they gave free rein to their primitive instincts to assault any woman who crossed their path. Once they had finished with one girl, one of them shouted out, "There's another one," and everyone repeated after him, "Another one, another one," and they all rushed off to their new victim. This hysterical form of mass aggression is merely a rehearsal for the total chaos that could break out anywhere at any moment. There were reports on the Internet that what happened in central Cairo was repeated in the Delta towns of Zagazig and Mansoura over the Eid. Without doubt the young men who took part in this mass assault to satisfy their sexual appetites would turn at the first opportunity to plunder, looting, and arson.

Second, the sexual frenzy that overwhelmed these young men is not just an expression of sexual frustration. Sexual desire can often have buried within it feelings of despair, frustration, injustice, insignificance, and futility, and all of these are common among the poor in Egypt. These young men are the children of destitute, broken people who die of kidney failure or are poisoned by drinking sewage water, people who have cancer from Youssef Wali's pesticides, people who burn to death in trains to Upper Egypt or drown on the ferries of death. They do not care if they live or die. These rampaging young men are the children of unemployment, impotence, and overcrowding. They live crammed into tiny rooms in buildings without utilities or public services. They have lost all hope for the future, hope of work, of marriage, or even of emigration abroad. They live without dignity, and any policeman can detain them, beat them, and abuse them. What is striking is that when they assaulted their victims, these young men used the same methods the police and State Security personnel use with the wives of detainees and suspects to extract their confessions. This frenzied and hysterical behavior no doubt contains a large dose of revenge against an ugly and hostile reality that does not provide the minimal conditions for a decent life. These young men, when they commit these communal acts of sexual assault, might well be taking revenge on those responsible for their wretched and degrading lives.

Third, if such an act of mass sexual assault took place in the West, many would hurry to accuse western society of decadence and moral decay. When it happens in Egypt, it means the religiosity so prevalent today is superficial and without substance. For centuries Egypt had its own understanding of Islam, a tolerant and open-minded understanding compatible with the civilized nature of Egyptians. Egypt always managed, in quite an unusual way, to preserve its form of Islam with its openness to the world, and Egyptian women were the first in the Arab world to be educated, to work outside the home, and to win society's respect as human beings with rights equal to those of men, at least until the end of the 1970s, when Egyptian society was subjected to a sweeping invasion of Wahhabi ideas from Saudi Arabia. One factor that led to this invasion is that President Anwar Sadat used religion to overcome the leftist opposition, and the Mubarak regime continues to support Wahhabism in order to benefit from the political submissiveness it installs in people's minds. Another is that the price of oil increased several times over after the October 1973 war, giving Saudi Arabia more influence than it ever had before and enabling it to impose its understanding of Islam on Egypt and the Arab world. As corruption and despotism added to poverty in Egypt, millions of Egyptians flocked to work in the Gulf, and came back years later with money and Wahhabi ideas. Sectors of Egyptian society acquired Saudi customs and forms of behavior previously unknown in Egypt, such as the *niqab*, beards, white gowns, closing shops at prayer time, taking one's shoes off when going into a house, and so on.

In reality the Wahhabi ideology sees women as merely vessels for sex, a source of temptation, and a means to produce children. What preoccupies the Wahhabis most is covering up women's bodies and preventing them as far as possible from mixing in society, in order to ward off the evil of their allure. This debased view of women strips them of their identity as human beings and considers them to be merely females. It believes that women have no willpower and such a weak sense of honor that to be alone with one inevitably leads to sin. In the eyes of Wahhabis a woman is not fully competent; she cannot drive or wander around alone without a man to protect her from abduction or rape. Although these ideas purport to promote virtue, in the end they lead to a view of women as sexual prey who cannot say no or defend themselves. The man has to protect a woman from others, but if he can obtain access to other men's women and escape punishment then he will not hesitate. Remember that in Saudi Arabia abducting and raping women and children is a frightening phenomenon and a real danger. Now we can see how until the end of the 1970s Egypt, open-minded and moderate, showed true religiosity in behavior and social relations, whereas now, sullen and strict about the externals of religion, the country is far removed from the spirit of Islam. All it has is a veneer, contracted like an infection from Bedouin societies that are closed, backward, and hypocritical.

This tragedy has revealed that the Ministry of Interior no longer considers protecting people to be one of its duties. The police forces that search Egyptians and hold them up in the streets for hours simply because a member of President Mubarak's family or one of his ministers happens to be passing in a motorcade, the security agencies that abused, beat, assaulted, and dragged along the ground people who demonstrated in favor of democracy and the independence of the judiciary, all this vast apparatus of repression never thought of sending forces to secure the downtown area during the Eid holiday. In fact several policemen and a young officer appear in pictures of the incident, completely indifferent to the carnival of sexual assault raging in front of their eyes. One policeman acted as instinct should have dictated, just one policeman whose sense of honor impelled him, on his own initiative, to take off his belt and try to beat back the frenzied hordes with it. But his courage counted for nothing against their numbers and against their determination to ravage another victim. In fact the comments by the Interior Ministry on the disaster, both on the television program Ten PM and in the government newspapers, were contradictory and to a large extent inept. They denied what happened and said Kasr al-Nil police station had not received any reports of sexual assault, as though a policeman's duty is merely to sit in a police station and wait for reports to arrive. We would like to ask Interior Minister Habib al-Adli: What would have happened if these sex-crazed young men, whom your officers left to assault Egyptian women for a full four hours, had instead been chanting slogans against President Hosni Mubarak? Would not an army of riot police have been deployed immediately to crush them? Is protecting President Mubarak from hostile chants more important to you than protecting the honor of Egyptian women?

What happened in central Cairo shows that the great collapse has already begun. Egypt is falling apart while President Mubarak, who has ruled the country for a quarter of a century and has brought it to rock bottom, is interested only in handing the country over to his son. We all have a duty to act to save our country from the bleak future that looms on the horizon, and the only way to save Egypt is through a real democracy that restores to Egyptians their humanity, their rights, and their dignity, as well as their civilized behavior.

November 5, 2006

Why Do Egyptians Harass Women?

The traditional answer to this question is that, although women are the victims of sexual harassment, they are themselves to blame because they wear tight or skimpy clothes that excite young men and impel them to harass women. This explanation contains a major fallacy and twisted logic: it implies that women must always take the blame, even for misconduct and crimes of which they are the victims, and that young men are merely animals unable to control their instinctive urges, such that whenever a woman in tight clothes comes into sight they pounce on her and rape her. But this argument, which unfairly blames the victim, has recently fallen apart, exposed as completely baseless. Studies have shown that more than 75 percent of the women subjected to sexual harassment in Egypt are women who wear the *hijab*. In fact video footage available on the Internet of an incident of mass sexual harassment in central Cairo two years ago shows the harassers groping a woman who is wearing the *isdal*, which covers the whole body. Besides, until the end of the 1970s it was socially acceptable in Egyptian society for a woman to wear a swimsuit that exposed parts of her body to men, and beaches and swimming pools in clubs all had girls and women going into the water in swimsuits without anyone harassing them. In fact the fashions prevalent at that time, such as the miniskirt, exposed a woman's legs, and many women in Egypt would wear such clothes at work, at college, and on public transport. At the time short skirts aroused the disapproval of conservatives but they never encouraged people to harass women.

So it's certain that sexual harassment is an intrusive disease that did not exist as a phenomenon thirty years ago, and that tight or skimpy clothing is in no way the stimulus for sexual harassment. The phenomenon of sexual harassment in Egypt, which has spread in recent times, undoubtedly has many social and economic dimensions. There is sexual repression, the late marrying age, unemployment, poverty, the prevalence of unregulated housing, frustration, empty lives, and a sense of unfairness. In my opinion these are all important but contributing factors, while the root cause in my view is a change in the way we see women. Throughout human history there have been two ways to think of women. There is the civilized way, where the woman is seen as a human being who happens to be female, just as a man is a human being who happens to be male. This civilized view of women acknowledges all of women's human abilities and capacities, not just their femininity, so it leaves plenty of space for respectful human interaction. With this view, men deal with their female colleagues and female students or teachers at university as human beings and not just as women they want to sleep with. The retrogressive view of women is that they are only bodies desired by men, that women are first and last female, instruments of pleasure, sources of temptation, and machines for producing children, and that a woman's activities, other than her functions as a woman, are secondary and marginal. The truth is that Egyptian society made great and early strides toward modernization starting in the nineteenth century, and so Egyptians very early acquired a civilized attitude of respect for the status of women as human beings. Egyptian women were pioneers in the Arab world, the first to be educated, the first to take employment, the first to drive cars and fly planes, the first to sit in parliament, and the first to hold ministerial positions.

A civilized view of women as human beings prevailed in Egypt until the beginning of the 1980s, when the country was swept by a powerful wave of fundamentalist Wahhabi thinking that offered a completely different view of women. In the eyes of the fundamentalists a woman meant a body first and last, and their main concern was to cover that body up. A few days ago a prominent Saudi sheikh called on Muslim women to wear the *niqab* with one eye opening, to keep themselves safe from furtive glances and to protect morality. This view of women as just bodies inevitably turns women into sexual prey vulnerable to attack at any time. It sees women as creatures almost without moral willpower that must always be accompanied by male relatives to protect them from others and from themselves. Seeing women as just bodies disposes harassers toward targeting them as soon as the harassers feel immune from punishment.

The regressive view of women, which is now spreading in Egypt, was unfortunately imported from desert nomadic societies that are far behind Egypt in every field of human activity. Instead of us helping those societies to progress, we have been infected by their backward ideas. The young men who come out on public holidays to harass women in the street are simply applying what they have learned about women, because, if a woman is just a body, if she represents only lust and pleasure, if she is a source of temptation, then why wouldn't one molest her whenever one is sure of impunity? The Egyptian newspaper *al-Masry al-Youm* interviewed some of the harassers and they all claimed that any women who went out for a walk on a public holiday wanted young men to harass them. This logic is completely in line with the backward fundamentalist view of women: that women carry temptation in their blood, even if they pretend the opposite, that men must guard their women with extreme vigilance, and that any woman who goes out alone when it is crowded is no more than a fallen woman who wants young men to harass her. We have replaced our civilized view of women with a regressive view cloaked in religion in a way that has no basis in religion, and we have started to pay a heavy price for these backward ideas.

Before we urge young men not to harass women, we first have to teach them how to respect women. We have to stop discussing what women must wear and what they can take off, whether they have to cover their ears or can leave locks of hair hanging down. We have to abandon that backward view, which is in fact obsessed with women's bodies even when its advocates pretend to be pious and call for women to be covered. We have to restore our civilized Egyptian ideas and remember that women are mothers, sisters, and daughters, the complete equals of men in abilities, rights, and duties. We have to show these young men examples of women's professional success and intellectual distinction. They have to know about women doctors, engineers, and judges. Then they will realize that women have real abilities that are much more important than their bodies, and only then will they stop harassing women in the street.

October 22, 2008

How Should We Overcome
the Temptation Posed by Women?

D ear reader,
Imagine that one day you go to your place of work and find
all your colleagues wearing masks. You can hear their voices but
you cannot see their faces. How would you feel? Of course you wouldn't
feel at ease and if the situation continued it would make you nervous,
because we always need to see the faces of those we are talking to. Human
communication is complete only when faces are visible. That has been the
nature of mankind since the beginning of creation. But those who force
women to cover their faces do not understand this fact.

In the aftermath of the 1919 uprising against the British occupation,
the pioneering Hoda Shaarawi took the Turkish burka off her face at a public ceremony as a sign that the liberation of the country was inseparable
from the liberation of women. Egyptian women were truly the pioneers
for women in the Arab world: the first to be educated and to work in
every field, the first to drive cars and fly planes, and the first to enter parliament and government. But at the end of the 1970s Egyptians fell under
the influence of fundamentalist ideas and the Wahhabi school of thought
proliferated, with the support of oil money, whether through satellite television channels owned by fundamentalists or through the millions of poor
Egyptians who worked for years in Saudi Arabia and came home saturated
with fundamentalist ideas. From then on, the *niqab*, or full face-veil, began
to reappear in Egypt—a phenomenon that requires an objective debate.
It's a difficult question because those who advocate the *niqab* are usually
fanatical extremists quick to accuse those who oppose them of calling for

licentiousness and decadence. This logic is naïve and mistaken, because the choice for humans has never been between the *niqab* and licentiousness, and between the two of them there are many varieties of balanced behavior. The question here is whether the *niqab* protects men from the allure of women and promotes virtue? To answer this question, we have to bear in mind several facts.

Islam never required women to cover their faces. Otherwise, if we could not see any part of a woman's face in the first place, why would God tell us to avert our eyes? In early Muslim society, women took part in public life, studying, working, trading, acting as nurses during times of war, and sometimes taking part in the fighting. Islam respected women and gave them rights equal to those of men. Women were oppressed only when Muslims were going through decadent times. Several months ago, the senior ulema of al-Azhar compiled a book distributed by the Ministry of Religious Endowments and entitled *al-Niqab 'ada wa-laysa 'ibada* (The Niqab is a Custom, not a Form of Worship). They show with evidence drawn from *sharia* that the *niqab* does not have the slightest connection with Islam. I do not believe that anyone can challenge these eminent scholars in their knowledge of Islamic precepts.

Given that wearing the *niqab* is not a divine injunction, we have a right to ask questions about its advantages and disadvantages. All ancient societies required women to cover their faces because they considered women a source of temptation and thought that vice could be prevented only by isolating and secluding them. This argument assumes that men will fall into temptation simply by seeing the face of a beautiful woman. This denies a man's capacity to control his instincts. Besides, if women must cover their faces so as not to arouse men, what should a handsome man do? Doesn't his handsome face equally arouse women? Should we require handsome men to cover their faces, so that men and women both wear the *niqab*? We also find that the eyes of a woman who wears the *niqab*, if they are beautiful, become themselves a powerful source of allure. So what should we do then to prevent arousal? A well-known Saudi religious scholar, Sheikh Mohamed al-Hadban, has thankfully understood this problem and advocated that Muslim women wear a *niqab* which reveals only one eye, so that women cannot possibly arouse men by the way they look. I do not know how these poor women could go about their lives, looking out on the world with one eye through a single hole.

The *niqab* prevents women from living as human beings with rights and obligations equal to those of men. How could a woman work as a surgeon, a judge, an engineer, or a television broadcaster when she is hidden behind the *niqab*, whether with one eye or two eyes uncovered? Most Saudi scholars strongly oppose women driving cars, presenting three arguments for this position: women would immodestly have to take off the *niqab* while driving; they would be able to go wherever they want, which would encourage them to rebel against their husbands and their families; and (according to Sheikh Muhammad ibn Salih al-'Uthaymin) "women are by nature less decisive than men, have weaker sight and are less capable, and if they face danger, are unable to respond." This is the real view of the advocates of the *niqab* and it indicates that they despise women and have contempt for their abilities. Of course they are unable to explain the overwhelming superiority women have achieved in education and employment throughout the world.

The most serious aspect of the *niqab* is that it dehumanizes women. Throughout human history there have been two attitudes toward women: the civilized attitude, which sees women as fully competent and qualified human beings, and the regressive attitude, which can be summarized as seeing her as feminine and hence limited to the role of acting as a source of sexual pleasure, as a factory for producing children, and as a maid in the conjugal home. These three roles are linked to a woman's body rather than her intellect, and hence for them the woman's body acquires supreme importance, while her intellect, her education, and her work, even her thoughts and feelings, are secondary, if taken into account at all.

Advocates of the *niqab* believe that to let men and women mix leads necessarily to temptation and vice, and so the only remedy for this state of affairs is to segregate the two genders completely and to make women cover their faces. If this argument is valid, then Saudi society must have done away with vice completely and forever because in Saudi Arabia segregation is total and all women are obliged to wear the *niqab*. In fact Saudis have a large organization called the Association for the Promotion of Virtue, which works day and night to monitor people's behavior and punish them as soon as they commit the slightest moral misdemeanor. But has virtue been achieved in Saudi Arabia? Studies and statistics affirm the opposite. One study, by Dr. Wafaa Mahmoud of King Saud University, found that a quarter of Saudi children between the ages of six and twelve were victims of sexual harassment. Another study by Dr. Ali al-Zahrani, a specialist in psychiatric diseases at the Saudi Ministry of Health, has corroborated this finding.

Dr. Khaled al-Halibi, the director of the Family Development Center in the Saudi province of Ahsa, conducted a study and found that 82 percent of the secondary schoolchildren he surveyed had suffered from forms of sexual deviance and that in one year alone (2007) 850 Saudi girls ran away from their families because of assault within the family, mostly of a sexual nature, 9 percent of children were the victims of sexual abuse by their guardians, one in four girls in the Gulf were subjected to sexual harassment, and 47 percent of the children surveyed had received obscene invitations on their cell phones.

The communications revolution has given rise to a major social crisis in Saudi Arabia, as young men who are socially and sexually repressed have started to use the cameras on their cell phones for immoral purposes. In 2005, images taken by cell phone showing four young men trying to rape two women wearing the *niqab* in a Riyadh street were widely circulated in Saudi Arabia. The question is how could a young man try to rape a woman when he could not see her body or her face? The answer is that as far as he was concerned she was not a human being but a body, just a sexual object, and if he could enjoy her while escaping punishment then he would not hesitate for a moment. In short the state of Saudi society with regard to sexual deviance and assault is no better than that of other societies, if not worse.

So finally, if the *niqab* does not bring out virtue, what is to be done? How can we overcome the temptation posed by women? The reality is that virtue never comes about through prohibitions, seclusion, and repression but rather through upbringing, setting an example, and willpower. When we see women as human beings with moral volition, dignity, and independent personalities, when we recognize their rights, as endorsed in Islam, when we trust and respect women and give them a full opportunity to be educated and to work, only then will virtue come about.

Democracy is the solution.

July 21, 2009

The Niqab and Flawed Religiosity

L
ast week I wrote an article about the phenomenon of the *niqab* now spreading in Egypt, ninety years after Egyptian women first abandoned it. I said that Islam does not require women to cover their faces at all, based on the opinion of a group of al-Azhar scholars who wrote a book entitled, *al-Niqab 'ada wa-laysa 'ibada* (The Niqab is a Custom, Not a Form of Worship), distributed by the Egyptian Ministry of Religious Endowments. Many other Egyptian jurists have endorsed this opinion, foremost among them Sheikh Mohamed Abduh (1849–1905) and Sheikh Mohamed Ghazali (1917–96), the great and courageous scholar who fought vehemently against what he called "the law of the Bedouin," which aims to segregate women behind the *niqab*. I tried to explain the negative effect of the *niqab* on women and society and cited as an example Saudi society, in which all women are forced to wear the *niqab*. I also cited official Saudi statistics showing that, with respect to sexual assault and forms of sexual deviance, Saudi society is no better, and possibly worse, than other societies, and thus that imprisoning women behind the *niqab* does not prevent vice.

After the article was published, I opened the *al-Shorouk* website and found to my surprise that the website was flooded with dozens of messages from advocates of the *niqab*. Unfortunately the messages did not contain a single argument for debate but rather tried their best to insult and abuse my person, without addressing in the slightest my opinion and the opinions of the jurists I quoted. In the face of these ferocious and vulgar attacks on me, a large group of readers sprang to my defense, and I take this opportunity to thank them from my heart and to take pride in their trust and their appreciation. The truth is that these insults did not bother me because as a physician I have learned in surgery that the process of opening an abscess with a scalpel, while essential for the health of the patient, necessarily involves malodorous pus coming out. We are dealing here with a phenomenon that truly deserves to be pondered, because those who competed with each other to insult me are supposed to be religious—in fact they consider themselves more committed than others to their religion—and this provides an excellent opportunity to study their way of thinking.

I noticed first of all that they believe with complete assurance that Islam has only one form, one opinion, and one worldview. Everything that contradicts their opinion has nothing to do with Islam, and anyone who opposes their opinion is either ignorant, degenerate, or conspiring against Islam on behalf of foreign forces. So they consider it their duty not to debate their opponents but rather to dismiss them, insult them, and disparage them, if possible, because they are enemies or conspirators, not just people with different points of view. The truth is that nothing is further from true Islam than this extremist and unilateral approach, because Islam is the only religion that requires its adherents to believe in other religions. Muslims have surprised the world over seven centuries with their ability to accommodate other cultures and integrate them into Islam's great civilization.

Second, they expect you to agree with them when they imprison women behind the *niqab*, or at least to refrain from objecting. If you do object they immediately accuse you of advocating nudity and pornography. They consider the *niqab* to be the only alternative to decadence. We have to wonder how these people view women who do not wear *hijab* and how they deal with them, let alone how they view Copts, and what image of Islam they offer to foreigners if they live in western countries.

Third, they are practicing a form of piety based not on any intrinsic spiritual experience but rather on comparison and discrimination. In their view the way to religious virtue is not through disciplining themselves to do good works and suppressing their desires but rather through advertising their religious superiority over others. From their differences they acquire a psychological strength that leads them to arrogance and presumption. They imagine that they alone are truly devout and that others face two options: either to accept their ideas without discussion or face their curses and insults. They live in a delusional world that spares them the trouble of thinking about their real problems. The world for them is made up of two camps: Muslims, who have to share their opinions in every detail, and the camp of Islam's enemies, including secularists, infidels, and degenerates. This bipolar vision, in its naivety and extremism, easily pushes them toward hatred and aggression, rather than toward love, tolerance, and the acceptance of differences—the values that true religion advocates.

Fourth, I noticed that most of their messages are full of horrendous grammatical and linguistic errors, and I concluded from this that they have acquired their religious learning by listening rather than by reading, mostly from satellite television channels subsidized by oil money that aim to propagate Wahhabi fundamentalist ideas. I watched one of these channels yesterday and found the famous preacher recounting the following incident: "The Prophet Muhammad was invited to someone's house and ate all the food served to him except the onions. When his host asked him why, the Prophet said he did not eat raw onions in case the angels were repelled by the smell of his breath when they were bringing him revelations." This is the level of the religious education these channels instill in the minds of simple people, and I do not think that requires any further comment.

Fifth, I have noticed that religion for them is purely a matter of formal ritual, requiring specific procedures, and so these devout people see no contradiction between insulting people and being devout. This flawed religiosity, which separates belief from conduct, is spreading like a plague in our country. Nowadays we find many people who are scrupulous about the rituals of religion, but as soon as we have to deal with them in mundane matters we discover that that their conduct belies appearances. Unfortunately in Egypt we have become more scrupulous about the externals of religion and yet less religious. Before Wahhabi ideas started spreading we were less interested in the externals of religion and more religious in the real sense—more just, more honest, and more tolerant.

Finally, the most dangerous aspect of this flawed religiosity is that it completely separates the private from the public. Those who bombarded the *al-Shorouk* website with insults imagined that in this way they were defending Islam. Yet they live in Egypt, where millions of people are impoverished, unemployed, ignorant, and diseased, where people die standing in bread lines or fighting to obtain clean water. But their flawed religiosity prevents them from making an objective analysis of any phenomenon, because in their opinion poverty is either a punishment or God's choice and they can never see it as the natural result of corruption or despotism. Besides, this flawed religiosity is totally depoliticized, because these people have learned from Wahhabi sheikhs that it is their duty to obey a Muslim ruler, even if he is unjust or corrupt. This leads them to accept despotism. They come out in angry demonstrations in protest at the French government's decision to ban the *hijab* in French schools, while in their own countries elections are regularly rigged and tens of thousands of detainees, mostly Islamists, spend the flower of their youth in prison without trial. Egyptians are abused and cruelly tortured and their wives may be abused in front of their eyes in police stations and at State Security premises. But none of that arouses their religious anger because the religion they have been taught does not include defending general human values, such as freedom, equality, and justice. Resisting injustice and despotism in Egypt is a costly exercise through which you may lose your freedom, your dignity, and perhaps your life, whereas hiding behind a fictitious name and slandering people on the Internet is an easy form of struggle and costs nothing.

This experience has confirmed to me once again that there are two battles in Egypt: a battle to bring about democratic reform, to prevent the transfer of power from President Mubarak to his son (as though the country were a poultry farm), and to assert the right of Egyptians to freedom and justice, and another parallel battle of no less importance, in which Egypt is defending its civilized and open-minded interpretation of Islam against the invasion of reactionary and regressive Wahhabi ideas that are liable to obliterate our cultural heritage and turn our great country into a Taliban emirate.

Democracy is the solution.

July 28, 2009

Piety in Front of the Camera

In the 1960s there was an al-Azhar sheikh in my family by the name of Sheikh Abdel Salam Sarhan, a man of awesome appearance with his great stature, his al-Azhar garments, and his stentorian voice. We who were children at the time loved him because his pockets were always full of chewing gum, which he would share out among us. When people needed his opinion on any legal matter, he would receive them hospitably in his house and explain the rules of Islam to them. It was out of the question at the time that Sheikh Abdel Salam would ever charge any fee for his efforts. In fact all he asked of people is that they pray for him and his family. What I learned from Sheikh Abdel Salam, may he rest in peace, is that a real man of religion is a great personality no less worthy of respect than a doctor or a judge. I also learned that making people aware of the precepts of their religion is the true vocation of the ulema, although Sheikh Abdel Salam's time has passed, Egypt has changed, and a new generation of preachers has arisen, different in every respect. Since Egyptians are naturally devout and increasingly resort to God because of the poverty, injustice, and humiliation they face in this world, since there are millions of illiterate people and even the educated find it hard to access the original sources of Islam, the new preachers have become the main source of religious learning for millions of Egyptians, and hence play a decisive role in shaping public awareness. For this reason we should take a close look at this phenomenon to understand its nature.

First, most of these preachers do not have any academic training in the religious sciences and so their success is not the result of any deep knowledge of religion so much as of their persuasiveness and their personal appeal. That's why they are so careful to be neat and elegant and to use simplified everyday language to reach as large an audience as possible. In just ten years the new preachers have become a basic element in the commercial media market, in every sense of the word, and the fees they demand depend on the amount of advertising their programs generate. This of course increases as the size of the audience grows and the best-paid preachers are those whose programs generate the most advertising revenue. Suffice it to say that their fees last year ranged from 150,000 to a million Egyptian pounds a month, and some have devised new ways to sell their advice on matters of Islamic law, such as the Islamic phone line and escorting rich people on the *hajj* and the *umra* for outrageous fees. *Forbes Magazine* of the United States has published the incomes of some of these preachers and they are enormous. Of course we would like everyone to enjoy great wealth but we should remember that the Prophet Muhammad lived poor and died poor and that his companions never made money out of preaching, but rather spent money on spreading the message of Islam. Throughout Islamic history, calling people to God has never been a way to make a fortune. When I imagine how millions of poor Egyptians who live in shantytowns and cemeteries gather around the television to watch people talk to them about religion and then at the end of the month these wretched people are just as they were, while the bank balances of the preachers have grown by a million pounds, I can't countenance the contradiction.

Second, many of the new preachers rely on exciting the religious feelings of the audience during the program. This climaxes when the preacher starts weeping and makes the audience weep in fear of God. Another contradiction is striking here. Everyone who has appeared on television knows that dealing with the various cameras during the recording session requires preparation and expertise. With full respect, I wonder how the preacher manages to handle simultaneously the strong religious emotions that make him weep and the need to pay attention to the cameras and their movements, which requires him to turn rapidly from one camera to another, based on the instructions of the producer.

Third, the discourse these preachers offer deals only with formalities and rituals: the *hijab*, prayer, fasting, the *hajj*, and the *umra*. Of course I have no objection to that, but they never speak about freedom, justice, or equality—the humane principles Islam was originally revealed to put into practice. The idea they convey to the world is that moral virtues are the only remedy for human suffering, whereas in fact promoting moral virtues is in no way sufficient to bring about justice. The millions of Egyptians who are mired in despair and degradation are first and foremost the victims of a corrupt and oppressive authoritarian system. That is the cause of their misery, and their suffering cannot be ended without a change in their conditions. One of these preachers has coined a well-known saying: "When as many people pray the dawn prayer as go to Friday prayers then Jerusalem will be liberated." Yet we see the number of people praying in. Egypt constantly increasing while they ceaselessly suffer defeat and disaster after defeat and disaster, because God will not change the state we are in unless we work to change it. Prayers alone are not enough.

Fourth, this reading of religion, which absolves the regime in power from its responsibility and makes people live with injustice instead of rising up against it, is exactly what explains why the security agencies favor the new preachers. In his important book, *Zahirat al-du'at al-judud* (The Phenomenon of the New Proselytizers), Professor Wael Lotfi has shown that all of them, without a single exception, operate in full cooperation with the security agencies, in the sense that they agree in advance with security officials on what can be said and what cannot be said, whether on television or in the mosques. All of us remember how these preachers all opposed the demonstrations organized in Egypt in solidarity with the Palestinians and the Iraqis. They called on people, instead of demonstrating, to pray and fast. That's what their agreement with the security agencies required, and the preacher would pay a high price for any violation of the agreement, ranging from a ban on preaching to expulsion from Egypt, as recently happened to one of them.

Fifth, Muslim jurists disagree on whether it is legitimate to take fees for issuing *fatwa*s. Some consider it legitimate as long as the fee comes through the government while others allow it as long as the jurist receives only as much as he and his family need. The famous medieval jurist, Ahmad ibn Hanbal, insisted that anyone who issues *fatwa*s should be rich enough not to need payment. The idea here is that the man of religion is like a judge who adjudicates in disputes and so he should have the same independence as a judge, but many Egyptians, including me, hold it against the ulema of al-Azhar that they are civil servants appointed by the state, which compromises their neutrality and can place them in a predicament if they issue a ruling that contradicts the wishes of the state. We have to extrapolate in the case of the new preachers, who receive their ample income from satellite television channels owned by people or institutions, mostly Saudi—a fact that could definitely affect their neutrality in matters related to the interests of the owners. This was blatantly obvious during the last Israeli war on Lebanon, when most Arabs and Muslims supported Hezbollah and took pride in its triumph, while the position of the traditional Saudi government was against Hezbollah and Iran. This put the new preachers in a difficult position. While Israeli war planes were using bombs that are internationally banned and that burned the skin of Lebanese children, most of the new preachers held their tongues. One of them waited a full three weeks before issuing a bland statement in which, as usual, he called on Muslims to pray. He then described the victims in Lebanon as "the dead," rather than as "martyrs," in line with the Saudi attitude toward Shi'ites.

The phenomenon of new preachers in this form plays a fundamental role in holding back the change we look forward to seeing in Egypt. When we ask why Egyptians do not rise up against injustices that would suffice to bring about revolution in some countries, we have to understand that the existence of injustice, or even awareness of injustice, is not enough to bring about revolution. What brings about revolution is awareness of the causes of injustice, so everything that prevents people from being aware of their rights becomes an instrument in the hand of despotism.

Democracy is the solution.

August 2, 2009

What Will Protect the Copts?

For years I worked in the same clinic as a Coptic dentist and we quickly became friends. He was a good man, honest in his work and in his dealings with people, but like many Egyptians he was completely detached from public affairs and was not aware of most political events. As far as he was concerned, the limits of the world were his work and his family. Then the last elections came around and I was surprised to find him away from work. When I asked him why, he said he had gone to vote for President Mubarak. I thought that strange and I asked him, "Why did you vote when you know that these elections have been rigged, as usual?" After a brief pause, he answered with his usual candor, "Actually at church they asked us to vote for the president and they organized buses to take us there and bring us back." I remembered this story when I was reading the recent remarks by Pope Shenouda, who twice in one week has declared his support for Gamal Mubarak as the next president of Egypt. So it's now clear that the Egyptian Church endorses the idea that President Mubarak's son, Gamal, should inherit the presidency of our country from his father—a phenomenon that is unique in the history of Egypt and that merits some debate.

First, Pope Shenouda represents a spiritual rather than a political authority as the spiritual head of the Copts and not their political leader. So, with all due respect, I maintain that he is exceeding his authority when he speaks politically on behalf of the Copts, and if we are campaigning to set up a secular state in Egypt in which citizens have full rights regardless of their religion, that requires separating religion from politics—the complete opposite of what Pope Shenouda has done. He has used his religious status to impose his political position on the Copts, thereby usurping their right to express their political opinions, which may not necessarily match his opinion.

Second, no one elected the current regime in Egypt and Egyptians did not choose it through their own free will. The regime took power through repression, detentions, and rigging elections. Through its failed and corrupt policies it has thrown millions of Egyptians into misery. I have no doubt that Pope Shenouda, like all Egyptians, is aware of these facts. I take this opportunity to ask His Grace: Does it conform with the teachings of Christ that you should take the side of a corrupt and oppressive political system against the wishes of the people and their right to choose their rulers, that you should ignore the sufferings of the millions of victims of this regime, including those killed through negligence or corruption and those who live in inhumane conditions? Does it conform to the teachings of Christ that you should agree to the son inheriting the whole country from his father as though Egyptians were livestock or poultry? His Grace the Pope says that he does not support a hereditary system but that he predicts Gamal Mubarak will win the presidential elections. But we ask the Pope: You are well aware that the elections are all rigged, so why have you concealed this fact in your statements? Is hiding these facts in line with the teachings of Christ?

Third, Pope Shenouda is said to support despotism and the inheritance of power out of concern for the Copts, because he is worried that democracy would probably bring the Muslim Brotherhood to power. But the truth is that the regime has deliberately exaggerated the role and influence of the Muslim Brotherhood for use as a bogeyman against anyone who calls for democracy, and the more important truth is that despotism will never protect anyone from religious extremism, because religious extremism is one of the symptoms of despotism. Let us recall that at the peak of its power in 1950 the Brotherhood failed to obtain a single seat in parliament in the last free and fair elections before the revolution. The Wafd Party won by a landslide at the time, gaining a majority of seats as usual. The Brotherhood's electoral successes in recent years were not the result of their popularity but of people staying away from polling stations. If people turned out to vote, the Muslim Brotherhood would never win, but people will take part in elections only if they feel the voting will be free and fair. Fair elections, contrary to the Pope's fears, are what will eliminate the danger of religious extremism.

Fourth, Copts in Egypt are persecuted. This is a fact that cannot be denied. But Muslims are also persecuted. All the grievances of which the

Copts complain are valid, but if they looked around they would discover that these injustices afflict Muslims equally. Most Egyptians are deprived of justice, equality, equal opportunities, humane treatment, and their human rights, because Egyptians cannot take office unless they support the regime in power. There are two ways to relieve the Copts from oppression: either through them joining, as Egyptians, a national movement that seeks to achieve justice for all Egyptians, or through them dealing with the regime as a minority seeking sectarian privileges. This latter option is mistaken and extremely dangerous. Pope Shenouda's recent position, unfortunately, sends the regime the message that Copts favor despotism and the inheritance of power in exchange for the regime meeting their demands, as though the Pope were saying to President Mubarak, "Give us Copts the privileges we demand and then do what you like with the remaining Egyptians, because they are of no concern to us."

Fifth, this regrettable position on the part of Pope Shenouda is incompatible with the history of the Church he represents, for the patriotic history of the Copts is a real source of pride for every Egyptian. On the throne now held by Pope Shenouda there once sat a great man by the name of Pope Cyril V, who supported with all his strength the nationalist movement against British occupation and who had himself taken part in the 'Urabi Rebellion and the 1919 revolution. When nationalist leader Saad Zaghloul was in exile, all Egyptians boycotted the Milner Commission the British government had sent to contain the demands of the revolution. In order to incite sectarian strife, the British occupation appointed a Copt, Youssef Wahba Pasha, as prime minister in place of Saad Zaghloul. The patriotic Church at the time, after a single meeting, issued a statement dissociating itself from the position of Youssef Wahba and asserting that he represented only himself, whereas the Copts, like all other Egyptians, stood with the revolution and its leader. In fact a Coptic student from a wealthy family, Aryan Youssef Saad, threw a bomb at the motorcade of Prime Minister Youssef Wahba to give voice to the nation's protest at his betrayal. Al-Shorouk recently published the memoirs of Aryan Youssef and I hope Pope Shenouda finds time to read them so that he can be proud, as we are all proud, of the patriotism of the Copts.

Youssef Wahba Pasha was amazed when he discovered that the man who attacked his motorcade was a Copt like him, and he asked, "Why did you do that, clever guy?" Aryan replied without hesitation, "Because you went against the consensus of the nation, Pasha." Overnight Aryan Youssef became a national hero throughout Egypt, and when he was arrested and detained for questioning, all the officers and policemen referred to him as a hero. Even the prosecutor general, after questioning Aryan on a charge of throwing a bomb at the prime minister's motorcade, stood up at his desk, shook Aryan's hand, and embraced him, saying, "May God protect you, my child. You are a patriot who loves Egypt. This Egyptian spirit we must restore today so that we can accomplish what we wish for Egypt and what Egypt deserves of us." I hope His Grace Pope Shenouda understands that the aim of protecting Copts cannot be achieved by transforming them into a group separate from other Egyptians, in collusion with the despotic regime that oppresses and abuses people. This way of thinking is completely alien to the patriotic history of the Copts.

So what will protect the Copts? That will come about when they consider themselves Egyptians before Christians, and when they understand that their duty as Egyptians is to join the battle for a just state that treats all citizens equally, regardless of their religion. Justice alone will protect the Copts. They cannot demand justice for themselves to the exclusion of others, and they cannot obtain it alone at the expense of the Muslims. Justice must be achieved for all and justice comes about only through democracy, for democracy is the solution.

August 9, 2009

Egypt Sits on the Substitutes' Bench

I n the 1980s I obtained a master's degree in dentistry from the University of Illinois in the United States. The university required graduate students to study a number of subjects and then prepare theses to obtain their degrees. In exceptional circumstances the university would give outstanding students the opportunity to prepare their theses and do coursework at the same time. In the history of the histology department where I was studying, only two students at different times had been able to finish their master's in one year, and this achievement was greatly admired by all the Americans. These two students were Egyptian and their supervisor, Dr. Abdel Moneim Zaki, was also Egyptian.

Then I came back to Egypt and worked as a dentist in several places, including Torah Cement Company, where I discovered by chance that the company's cement laboratory played an important part in the history of Egypt. During preparations for the 1973 war, the company's chemists—Fakhry al-Daly, Nabil Gabriel, and others—worked to develop a special kind of cement in cooperation with the Egyptian Army Corps of Engineers. After arduous research they managed to produce a new, extra-strong cement with exceptional resistance to high temperatures, and Egyptian frogmen used this cement during the crossing of the Suez Canal to block napalm tubes in the Bar Lev line. When the Israelis opened the tubes to fire napalm, which would normally have turned the waters of the canal into a living hell, they were surprised by the improved Egyptian cement's ability to stop the burning napalm, even under heavy pressure. After that I read another story: The Bar Lev line was one of the most formidable military defenses in history and it was thought that only a nuclear bomb could demolish it, but an ingenious Egyptian engineer by the name of Major-General Baqy Zaky from the Army Corps of Engineers did a careful study of the line's composition, concluded that it was made of soil, and came up with an excellent, if simple, idea. He invented a water cannon that could increase water pressure until it had an extraordinary penetration capacity. During the crossing of the canal, Egyptian soldiers used the water cannon Baqy Zaky had invented on the Bar Lev line until it collapsed like a piece of cheese.

There is much to say about the ingenuity of Egyptians. Do you know the extent of Egyptian brain drain to Europe, America, and Australia? Some 824,000 Egyptians with advanced qualifications have gone abroad, a number equal to the population of some Arab countries, including three thousand scientists in important fields, such as nuclear engineering, genetics, and artificial intelligence. All of them would welcome the opportunity to serve their country. In the Gulf states the ingenuity of the Egyptians is most evident. These states, which acquire millions of dollars a day from oil, have built affluent new cities and set up giant companies. Egypt has succeeded in producing Ahmed Zewail, Magdi Yacoub, Naguib Mahfouz, Abdel Wahab, Umm Kulthum, and thousands of creative Egyptians, because the creativity of a people has nothing to do with wealth but rather with cultural experience accumulated over many generations. This cultural accretion exists in Egypt more than in any other Arab country, and in fact the Arab oil-producing countries are indebted to Egyptians in everything they have achieved. It was Egyptians who taught them at school and at university, who planned and supervised the construction of their cities, who set up radio and television stations, and who drafted their constitutions and their laws. You will find that even the national anthems of these countries were written and set to music by Egyptians.

Egyptian creativity is a fact that cannot be denied, so the question springs to mind: If Egypt has all this human creativity, why has it fallen to the back among the countries of the world, and why do most Egyptians live in misery? The reason can be summed up in one word: despotism. Egypt's talents will continue to be squandered and its potential will go to waste as long as the political system is despotic and oppressive. Public offices in Egypt always go to followers of the regime regardless of their competence or education. Office holders in Egypt are not interested in performance as much as in their image in the eyes of the ruler, because he is the only person who can dismiss them. Because most of them have no talent, they are hostile to those who are competent, whom they see as a threat to themselves and to their positions. The machinery of the Egyptian regime routinely excludes competent and talented people and opens the door to sycophants and cheerleaders. We may be the only country in the world where a minister who has failed in the field of housing takes responsibility for the oil sector, about which he knows nothing, simply because President Mubarak likes him, and the only country where someone is appointed prime minister when he has never attended a political meeting in his life.

The Egyptian people have never been tested, or only on a very few occasions, such as the War of Attrition, the October War, and the building of the High Dam. Every time they have been tested, Egyptians have passed the test with distinction, but afterward they go back to the substitutes' bench. We Egyptians are like a group of soccer players who are talented but whom the coach does not like, does not respect, and does not want to give a chance. Instead he uses a team of losers and degenerates who always bring the team to defeat. According to the rules of soccer a player who spends the whole season on the substitutes' bench has the right to revoke his contract. All of Egypt has been sitting on the substitutes' bench for thirty years, watching defeats and disasters and unable to intervene. Doesn't Egypt have the right, in fact the duty, to revoke its contract?

During my last visit to New York, I saw, as usual, many Egyptian university graduates working as restaurant waiters and as gas station attendants. One night I was walking down 42nd Street and I came across someone standing at a cart selling hot dogs. He looked Egyptian and I went up to him and spoke to him. I was surprised to find that he was a graduate of the Ain Shams medical faculty. He offered me mint tea and I sat in the street next to him. A customer came along and he got up to make him some hot dogs, and I thought I was seeing a living example of what the Egyptian regime is doing to Egyptians. This young man had worked hard and honorably to qualify for medical college, graduated as a doctor, and now he is making hot dogs for passersby. As though he were aware of my thoughts, he sat next to me, lit a cigarette, and said, "You know, sometimes I feel that my life's gone to waste. I'm afraid I'll spend my whole life making hot dogs in the street. But then I tell myself that here I'm a hot dog seller and a respected citizen, whereas in Egypt I might be a doctor but I would have no rights and get no respect." He told me how his father, a civil servant in the Ministry of Religious Endowments, had struggled to educate him and his sister; how after he graduated he discovered what he called the "three no's" theory—no job, no marriage, no future; and how he discovered that working in the Gulf was humiliating and uncertain, and that signing up for higher studies was beyond his means. He told me how he had asked the only girl he ever loved to forget him because he could not marry her or have her wait for him.

He paused a while and then, trying to be cheerful, he said, "Would you like to hear Mohamed Munir? I have all his tapes." He took a cassette player from his cart and added Munir's voice as background to the sad scene. It was bitterly cold and the heater next to the cart was inadequate. We pulled our coats tight around us and blew on our hands to little effect. The customers were gone and the street was almost empty but he would have to stay until morning, as the cart owner required. I stayed a long while with him, talking and laughing. Then I took my leave and he embraced me firmly. He did not speak. We didn't need to talk. I felt for him completely. I took a few steps away toward the square and did not look back, but he called after me in a loud voice. "Listen," he said. I turned around and found him smiling at me and saying, "Remember me to Egypt. I miss it very much."

Democracy is the solution.

August 25, 2009

Are Egyptians Really Religious?

For years I worked as a dentist in a large government establishment with thousands of workers. On the first day, while I was treating a patient, the clinic door opened and someone appeared. He introduced himself as Dr. Mahmoud, the pharmacist, and invited me to come and perform the noon prayer as part of a group. I declined, saying I would finish my work and then pray. We got into a discussion that almost became an argument because he insisted I abandon the patient and join the prayers, while I insisted on continuing to work. After that I discovered that Dr. Mahmoud's ideas were widespread among the people working in the establishment. They were as devout as can be. The women all covered their hair, and at least half an hour before the noon prayer everyone stopped work completely and set about performing ablutions and spreading mats in the corridors in preparation for communal prayers. Of course they would also take part in the *hajj* and *umra* trips the establishment organized every year. I had no objection to all that because it's a wonderful thing to be devout, but I quickly discovered that many of the people working there, although rigorous about performing their ritual obligations, were committing many serious offenses, ranging from mistreating people, lying, and hypocrisy to abusing subordinates and even taking bribes and embezzling public funds. In fact the Dr. Mahmoud who insisted on inviting me to prayers turned out later to have been tweaking the accounts and selling medicine on the side.

What happened in that establishment happens throughout Egypt: manifestations of piety are so widespread that a recent Gallup survey found that Egyptians are the most devout people on the face of the Earth. Yet at the same time Egypt leads the way in corruption, bribery, sexual harassment, fraud, and forgery. One has to wonder how we could be the most pious and the most delinquent at the same time. In 1664 the great French dramatist Molière wrote his play *Tartuffe*, about a corrupt man called Tartuffe who seeks to satisfy his basest desires while making a show of piety. At the time the Catholic Church raised a storm against Molière and prevented any performance of the play for a full five years. In spite of the ban *Tartuffe* become such a theatrical classic that the word Tartuffe is used in French and in English to refer to a hypocritical man of piety.

The question here is: Have millions of Egyptians become copies of Tartuffe? I think that the problem in Egypt is deeper than that. Egyptians really are devout, with a faith that is sincere, but many of them behave immorally without any pangs of religious conscience. Of course one must not generalize because there are many devout people in Egypt who are guided by their conscience in everything they do. The great judges who have fought for the independence of the judiciary to defend the dignity and freedom of Egyptians, jurist Noha al-Zeini who exposed the government's election rigging, Yahya Hussein who fought a fierce battle to protect public money in the Omar Effendi deal, and many others—all of these people are pious in the true sense. But on the other hand the young men who harassed women in the street on the morning of the Feast had fasted and prayed in Ramadan. The policemen who torture innocent people, the doctors and nurses who mistreat poor patients in public hospitals, the civil servants who rig the election results in the government's favor, and the students who cheat en masse, most of them are devout and rigorous about performing their ritual obligations. Societies fall sick in the same way as people, and our society is now suffering from a disconnect between belief and conduct, a disconnect between piety and ethics.

This sickness has numerous causes: first, the despotic regime, which necessarily leads to the spread of cheating, lying, and hypocrisy, and, second, the fact that the understanding of religion that now prevails in Egypt is ritualistic rather than behavioral, in the sense that it does not present religion as synonymous with morality but sees it as confined to the performance of a set of procedures, the completion of which qualifies one as pious. Some people will say that the formalities of worship are aspects of religion as important as morality. The fact is that all religions came about to defend human values—truth, justice, and freedom—and everything else is less important. The sad thing is that the Islamic tradition is full of evidence that ethics are the most important element of religion, but we do not understand that and we do not want to understand it. There's a well-known story about the time when the Prophet Muhammad met an ascetic who devoted himself to worship day and night, and the Prophet asked him, "Who provides for you?" The man answered, "My brother works and provides for me." Then the Prophet said, "Your brother worships more than you do." The meaning here is decisive and important: that someone who works and provides for his family is more virtuous in God's eyes than the ascetic who spends all his time worshiping but does not work.

A limited understanding of religion is one of the main reasons for the decline of conditions in Egypt. For twenty years the streets and mosques of Egypt have been filled with millions of posters urging Muslim women to wear the *hijab*. Imagine if these posters had urged people, on top of wearing the *hijab*, to reject the injustices imposed on Egyptians by the ruler, to defend the rights of detainees, or to prevent election rigging. If that had happened, democracy would have been established in Egypt and Egyptians would have extracted their rights from the despotic system.

Virtue can come about in only two ways: by real piety, which is completely identical to morality, or by morality alone, even if it is not based in religion. Some years ago my late mother fell ill with cancer and we called in one of the best cancer doctors in the world to treat her, Dr. Garcia-Giralt of the Curie Institute in Paris. This great scientist came to Egypt several times to treat my mother and then firmly refused to take any payment. When she insisted, he said, "My professional conscience does not permit me to take any payment for treating the mother of a fellow doctor." This man does not believe much in religion but his gracious and magnanimous behavior puts him at the highest level of real piety. I wonder how many of our great and devout doctors today would even think of refusing payment from a colleague.

Another example is an incident that took place in 2007. In order to improve the image of the Libyan regime around the world, an annual international literary prize was organized with a value of about $150,000 and with the name, Gaddafi International Prize for Literature. A committee of prominent Arab intellectuals was formed to choose a writer to receive the prize. That year the committee decided to award the prize to the great Spanish writer, Juan Goytisolo, who was seventy-eight years old. The surprise was that Goytisolo wrote a letter to the committee members thanking them for choosing him but also saying that he could not accept a prize from the Gaddafi regime, which had seized power in a military coup and had abused, through detention and torture, thousands of its opponents. Goytisolo turned down a prize worth $150,000 because it was incompatible with his moral conscience.

How many intellectuals or even men of religion in Egypt would turn down the prize? Which of them is closer to Almighty God: this high-minded Spanish writer, who I am confident never thought of religion when he took his brave and noble decision, or the dozens of devout Egyptians, Muslims and Christians, who cooperate with despotic regimes and put themselves at their service, completely ignoring the crimes these regimes perpetrate against their peoples? Real piety must go hand in hand with ethics because morality without piety is much better than piety without morality, and democracy is the solution.

August 31, 2009

The Sorrows of Miss Laurence

L aurence is a French woman, a physiotherapist who had the chance to work in Egypt and was overjoyed because, like most French people, she loved Egyptian civilization and dreamed of seeing the Nile, the pyramids, and the pharaonic temples. I met Laurence in Cairo on various occasions, but when I met her again a few days ago, I was surprised to hear her saying, "I've decided to leave Egypt forever."

"Why?" I asked.

"Because I can no longer stand being a woman on display," she answered.

"What do you mean?"

"Every time I go out in the street, I don't feel that I'm a human being with a mind and feelings. I feel that I'm just a body, because I'm a woman on display to everyone. Every man I meet looks at my body in an offensive manner and undresses me with his stares. I've started to avoid crowded places because I know that crowds mean harassment. They mean that a man's hand is going to reach out to my breasts or my legs or any part of my body."

"Does this always happen?" I asked.

"Invariably. If the guy can't touch me for the crowds, he speaks to me in broken English to ask if I have a boyfriend or a husband in an attempt to sleep with me. Even the men walking on the other side of the street shout out sexual remarks, or whistle or wave at me. A dozen men started to ogle my body simultaneously, and after that I started taking the women's carriage on the subway."

"Do you wear revealing clothes?" I asked.

"Not at all. You've seen me several times and you've seen what I wear. I respect the culture of others and I know that Egypt is a conservative country. Even in summer when I wear a sleeveless top, I always put on a silk shawl to cover my arms."

"Don't you get harassed like that in France?" I said.

"Very rarely. After a year and a half in Cairo I can't believe what's happening. Sometimes it seems like all Egyptian men have been struck with some sexual perversion. I've started to be afraid of going out in the street. If I don't have work I stay at home for whole days."

"What are you going to do now?" I asked.

"I'm happy to have found a job in Greece, and I'm impatient to leave. At least in Greece no one will try to grope me or ogle me or invite me to bed as soon as he sees me. There I'll feel like a human being and not a woman on show for sex."

My conversation with Laurence came to an end and I felt sad. How could this happen in Egypt, a country always known for being polite to foreigners and treating them well? I referred back to surveys carried out on sexual harassment in Egypt and I found some alarming results. Last year a survey by the Egyptian Center for Human Rights Education found that 98 percent of foreign women in Egypt had experienced sexual harassment. The strange thing is that this wave of harassment is spreading alongside an overwhelming wave of superficial religiosity. All these beards, *gallabiya*s, blaring loudspeakers, Salafist Wahhabi television channels, religious lessons, and manifestations of piety have not stopped the sexual harassment. Why do Egyptians harass women? The traditional answer is that the women themselves are responsible for the harassment because they wear revealing clothes and incite men to harass them. This is a perverse and incoherent argument, first, because it blames the victim instead of the perpetrator; second, because it portrays men as a bunch of stray beasts unable to control their instincts—as soon as they see a bare piece of a woman's body they pounce on her; third, because most women in Egypt now wear the *hijab* but this does not protect them from harassment, according to the survey I mentioned; fourth, because until the end of the 1970s Egyptian women wore very modern clothes that revealed their arms and legs but sexual harassment was much less common than it is now; and, fifth, because in France, for example, where women in general wear scanty clothing, the rate of sexual harassment is no more than 20 percent, according to the *New York Times*. This means that in pious Egypt, women suffer four or five times as much sexual harassment as women in secular France. In fact those societies that strictly segregate men and women, such as Saudi Arabia and Afghanistan, have the highest rates of sexual harassment in the world. The phenomenon in my opinion is much more complicated than the type of clothes women wear. My view is that sexual harassment is rampant is Egypt for several reasons.

One is unemployment. The millions of young men who have failed to find jobs after completing their education feel frustration and despair, and lose faith in the idea of justice, on the grounds that in Egypt causes do not lead to results. Hard work does not necessarily lead to success, academic excellence does not necessarily lead to a respectable job, and a commitment to morality does not necessarily lead to social advancement. In fact, on the contrary, moral deviance often leads to wealth. All this must push young men toward violence, and in this context psychologists say that sex crimes are not always committed in order to satisfy sexual desire and that men often engage in sexual harassment as a way to take revenge on society or to vent their anger and frustration.

Another is the difficulty of getting married in Egypt. Millions of Egyptians cannot afford to get married and, since traditions and religious injunctions (both Muslim and Christian) ban extramarital relations, most young Egyptians are sexually frustrated, which must sometimes lead them to harass women.

A third reason is the prevalence of pornographic videos and easy access to them because of the communications revolution and the spread of the Internet. In fact the harm done by pornographic material is not confined to arousing the instincts of the young, who are already repressed. It also normalizes and decriminalizes the idea of rape and removes the personal and respectful aspect of sexual relations, so that sexual harassment becomes merely an act of pleasure rather than an abhorrent crime.

The final reason is that our attitude toward women in Egypt has changed. At the beginning of the last century Egyptian women began a long struggle for liberation from the *harim*, for equality with men in education and employment, and for a respected position in society. Egyptian society then fell under the influence of the restricted Wahhabi reading of Islam. Although this reading is strict about covering up women's bodies, it also sees a woman as merely an instrument of pleasure, a source of temptation, a machine to produce children, and a house servant. Everything else is less important. In fact in their defense of Islamic dress codes, some Wahhabi sheikhs have likened women to pieces of candy that must be well wrapped so that flies don't land on them. This may be said with good intentions, but likening women to pieces of candy dehumanizes them because a piece of candy has no mind or feelings and its only purpose is to be eaten and enjoyed. So if someone wants some candy and cannot afford it, and if he has a chance to eat someone else's candy with impunity, he will not hesitate to take the chance. This is exactly what a man is doing when he sexually harasses women in the street.

The sexual harassment of women will not stop until we revive the true open-minded Egyptian reading of Islam, which sees women as human beings who are fully capable and competent, not just as bodies or pieces of candy. The harassment will stop when corruption, despotism, and injustice come to an end, when a new political system comes about, elected by the people, giving the millions of young people their natural right to live and work and get married.

Democracy is the solution.

September 13, 2009

Why Are Religious Fanatics Obsessed
with Women's Bodies?

The Shabaab movement in Somalia controls large parts of the south and center of the country, and because officials in this movement embrace the Wahhabi ideology they have imposed their views on Somalis by force and issued strict decrees banning films, plays, dancing at weddings, soccer matches, and all forms of music, even ring tones on cell phones. Some days ago these extremists carried out a strange operation: they arrested a Somali woman and whipped her in public because she was wearing a bra. They announced clearly that wearing these bras was un-Islamic because it is a form of fraud and deception. We may well ask what wearing bras has to do with religion, why they would consider them to be a form of fraud and deception, and how they managed to arrest the woman wearing the bra when all Somali women go around with their bodies completely covered. Did they appoint a special female officer to inspect the breasts of women passing by in the street? One Somali woman called Halima told Reuters news agency:

> Al Shabaab forced us to wear their type of veil and now they order us to shake
> our breasts. . . . They first banned the former veil and introduced a hard fabric
> which stands stiffly on women's chests. They are now saying that breasts
> should be firm naturally, or just flat.

In fact this excessive interest in covering up women's bodies is not confined to the extremists in Somalia. In Sudan the police examine women's clothing with extreme vigilance and arrest any woman wearing

111

trousers. They force her to make a public apology for what she has done and then they whip her in public as an example to other women. Some weeks ago Sudanese journalist Lubna al-Husseini insisted on wearing trousers and refused to make the public apology. When she refused to submit to flogging she was referred to a real trial and the farce reached its climax when the judge summoned three witnesses and asked them if they had been able to detect the shape of the accused's underwear when she was wearing the trousers. When one of the witnesses hesitated in answering, the judge asked him directly, "Did you see Lubna's stomach when she was wearing the trousers?" The witness gravely replied, "To some extent." Lubna said she was wearing a modest pair of trousers and that the scandalous pair she was accused of wearing would not suit her at all because she is plump and would need to lose 20 kilos in order to put them on. But the judge convicted her anyway and fined her 500 pounds or a month in prison.

In Egypt, too, extremists continue to take an excessive interest in women's bodies and in trying to cover them up entirely. They not only advocate that women wear the *niqab* but also that they wear gloves on their hands, which they believe will ensure that no passions are aroused when men and women shake hands. We really do face a phenomenon that deserves consideration: Why are extremists so obsessed with women's bodies? Some thoughts might help us answer this question.

First, the extremist view of women is that they are only bodies and instruments for either legitimate pleasure or temptation, as well as factories for producing children. This view strips women of their human nature. Accusing the Somali woman of fraud and deception because she was wearing a bra is the same as charging a merchant who conceals defects in his goods and makes false claims about their quality in order to sell them at a higher price. The idea here is that a woman who accentuates her breasts by using a bra gives a false impression of the goods (her body), which is seen as fraud and deception of the buyer (the man) who might buy (marry) her for her ample breasts and later discover that they were ample because of the bra and not by nature.

It would be fair to remember that treating women's bodies as commodities is not something found only in extremist ideologies but often happens in western societies, too. The use of women's naked bodies to market commercial products in the West is merely another application of the idea that women are commodities. Anyone who visits the red-light district in Amsterdam can see for himself how wretched prostitutes, completely naked, are lined up behind glass so that passersby can inspect their charms before agreeing on the price. Isn't that a modern-day slave market, where women's bodies are on sale to anyone willing to pay?

Second, extremists believe women to be the source of temptation and the prime cause of sin. This view, which is prevalent in all primitive societies, is unfair and inhumane, because men and women commit sin together and the responsibility is shared and equal. If a beautiful woman arouses and tempts men, then a handsome man also arouses and tempts women. But the extremist ideology is naturally biased in favor of the man and hostile to the woman, and considers that she is primarily responsible for all sins.

Third, being strict about covering up women's bodies is an easy and effortless form of religious struggle. In Egypt we see dozens of Wahhabi sheikhs who enthusiastically advocate covering up women's bodies but do not utter a single word against despotism, corruption, fraud, or torture because they know very well that serious opposition to the despotic regime (which should really be their first duty) would inevitably lead to their arrest and torture and the destruction of their lives. Their strictness on things related to women's bodies enables them to operate as evangelists without any real costs. Throughout human history, strictness toward women has usually been a way to conceal political abuses and real crimes. Somalia is a wretched country in the grip of famine and chaos but officials there are distracted from that by inspecting bras. The Sudanese regime is implicated in crimes of murder, torture, and raping thousands of innocents in Darfur but that does not stop the regime from putting on trial a woman who insists on wearing trousers. It is women rather than men who always pay the price for despotism, corruption, and religious hypocrisy.

Fourth, the extremist ideology assumes that humans are a group of wild beasts completely incapable of controlling their instincts, that it is enough for a man to see a bare piece of female flesh for him to pounce on her and have intercourse. This assumption is incorrect, because humans, unlike animals, always have the power to control their instincts by willpower and ethics. An ordinary man, if he is sane, cannot have his instincts aroused by his mother, sister, daughter, or even the wife of a friend, because his sense of honor and morality transcends his desires and neutralizes their effect. So virtue will never come about though bans, repression, and pursuing women in the street, but rather through giving children a good upbringing, propagating morality, and refining character. Societies that impose segregation between men and women (such as Afghanistan and Saudi Arabia) do not have lower rates of sexual crimes than other societies, according to official statistics. The rates there may even be higher.

We favor and advocate modesty for women but before all else we advocate a humane view of women, a view that respects their abilities, their wishes, and their thinking. What is really saddening is that the Wahhabi extremism spreading throughout the world with oil money, which gives Muslims a bad name, is as far as can be from the real teachings of Islam. Anyone who reads the history of Islam fairly has to be impressed by the high status it accords to women, because from the time of the Prophet Muhammad until the fall of Andalusia, Muslim women mixed with men, were educated, worked and traded, fought, and had financial responsibilities separate from their fathers or husbands. They had the right to choose the husband they loved and the right to divorce if they wanted. Western civilization gave women these rights many centuries after Islam. Finally, let me say that religious extremism is the other face of political despotism. We cannot get rid of the extremism before we end the despotism.

Democracy is the solution.

October 19, 2009

Nora and the National Squad

T his week I wanted to write about an Egyptian woman by the name of Nora Hashem Mohamed, but the great victory of our national soccer squad over Algeria cannot be ignored, so I decided to write about the two subjects together.

There's nothing special about Nora Hashem Mohamed. She's like millions of other Egyptian women: brown-skinned, moderately attractive, and poor. She's married to a simple laborer named Hani Zakaria Mustafa, with whom she has two boys and fights a daily battle to make a living and bring up the children. One day Nora suddenly felt ill.

The match between our soccer team and Algeria's was a battle of destiny during which the Egyptians showed their mettle, forgot their differences, and stood united behind the national team. When the Algerian media took part in some vulgar ridicule of the team, Egyptian commentators responded with a torrent of stinging insults, and when the Algerian singer, Warda, announced she would support the Algerian team, many Egyptians were angry and asked, "How dare Warda support the Algerian team when she's been living in Egypt and enjoying its bounty for decades?" Some Internet bloggers demanded that Warda be barred from Egypt to punish her for her failure to support our national team.

At first Nora attributed her exhaustion to lack of sleep and too much housework and she kept it a secret from her husband, Hani, so as not to add to his troubles. But her illness worsened until she took to her bed. At that stage Hani insisted on taking her to a private clinic and paid a doctor to examine her. The doctor advised that she be taken to the hospital immediately.

President Mubarak enthusiastically attended one of the national team's training sessions and spent time with the players to encourage them in the match. The truth is that President Mubarak is well-known for his patronage of sports. One might remember that when 1,400 Egyptians died in the famous ferry accident, the president's grief for the victims did not prevent him from attending a training session for another battle of destiny, in that case the final of the Africa Cup of Nations.

When Hani Zakaria and his wife, Nora, reached Imbaba Chest Hospital it was two o'clock in the morning. The doctor quickly examined Nora, said her condition was normal, and then left. Hani tried to discuss the case with him further but was not allowed to meet the doctor. Hani went back to the receptionist and begged him to help find treatment for his wife. The receptionist then told him straight that if he wanted his wife to be treated he must pay 2,000 Egyptian pounds right away.

During the match with Algeria, despite deliberate rough play on the part of the Algerians, our players displayed the highest level of self-control, and the deep piety of Egyptians was evident during and before the match. Millions of Egyptians prayed to God to have the Egyptian team score at least two goals and the singer, Ehab Tawfik, appeared on television, asking all the viewers to pray for the team and saying that in Egypt there are many righteous men whose prayers God would definitely answer.

Hani was amazed when he heard the amount of money required of him, and asked the receptionist in a soft voice whether Imbaba Chest Hospital was still a government hospital. The receptionist told him it was still a government hospital but he must nonetheless pay 2,000 pounds. Hani said he was poor and didn't have that amount of money. The receptionist didn't answer and proceeded to read some papers lying in front of him. Hani began to beg the receptionist to let his wife be treated.

On the morning of the day of the match, the well-known sports commentator, Yasser Ayoub, said on television that if the Egyptian team beat Algeria and qualified for the World Cup finals then every player on the team would receive a reward of six million pounds from the state and from the football federation. When the woman presenter showed signs of surprise at the amount, another sports commentator said the players on the national team would deserve more than that because they would have brought joy to the hearts of Egyptians.

When Hani despaired of persuading the receptionist at Imbaba Chest Hospital to help him, he took his wife, who was now staggering from exhaustion and fever, and went with her to Omrania Chest Hospital, where a doctor examined her and said he suspected she had swine flu.

He added that he couldn't treat her in the hospital because it was not equipped to deal with such cases, and advised Hani to take his wife to Umm al-Masriyyin Hospital, which did have the right facilities.

President Mubarak isn't the only sports enthusiast. His sons, Gamal and Alaa, share his passion and the two of them made sure they went to the stadium to support the national team. Most of the ministers and senior officials went along, too, including the health minister, who sat right next to Gamal Mubarak. We saw how happy they all were when Amr Zaki scored the first goal against Algeria.

Hani thanked the doctor, took his wife, Nora, and hurried to Umm al-Masriyyin Hospital, where he begged the officials to save his wife, who had started to spit blood, but the doctor there assured him that his wife's condition was normal and did not require hospitalization. He advised Hani to take her back to Omrania Chest Hospital because it specializes in such cases.

After the first goal, despite much effort and fighting spirit, our players were unable to score again for a full ninety minutes, and the faces of the senior officials sitting in their box showed exasperation. Alaa Mubarak could not control himself and even waved his hand in remonstration when our team missed a number of clear opportunities to score.

Hani retraced his steps, almost carrying his wife to Omrania Chest Hospital, and for the first time raised his voice in anger at the doctor. "Why did you send me to Umm al-Masriyyin Hospital when this is where she should be treated?" he asked. The doctor said that his diagnosis was correct and that the people at Umm al-Masriyyin Hospital avoided treating patients. He asked Hani for an official paper from Umm al-Masriyyin Hospital certifying that Nora's condition was normal and not serious. At that point Hani apologized to the doctor for his sharp words, took his wife back to Umm al-Masriyyin, and asked them for the document on his wife's condition. In fact this time they treated him kindly and said they would do the necessary tests for his wife, but he would have to come back at eight o'clock in the morning because the person responsible for testing was not at the hospital (it turned out later that she was there but felt overworked and had asked her colleagues to turn Nora away by whatever means possible).

The match was almost over and into extra time when Emad Moteab scored the second goal for Egypt and all of Egypt danced for joy. Dr. Hatem al-Gabaly, the minister of health, forgetting the dignity of his office and the fact that he was on live television, leapt from his seat and embraced Gamal Mubarak to congratulate him on the great victory.

Hani took his wife back to Omrania Chest Hospital to leave her there until morning, when he would come back and take her to do the tests at Umm al-Masriyyin. Nora's condition had deteriorated so much that she was put on an artificial respirator, and she drew her last breath before she was able to have the tests done to diagnose her condition. Nora Hashem Mohamed died before she reached the age of twenty-five, leaving a husband and two young boys. Perhaps we are the only country where people die this way, but the tragedy of Nora Hashem Mohamed should not mar the serenity of our joy at victory over Algeria. God answered our prayers and made sure we scored two clean goals. We made the Algerians taste defeat and, God willing, we will crush them in the next match. Congratulations to Egypt for reaching the World Cup and may God have mercy on the soul of Mrs. Nora Hashem Mohamed.

Democracy is the solution.

November 15, 2009

Defending Egypt's Flag

On November 14, 1935, Egypt was seething with protests against the British occupation and a large demonstration set off from Cairo University with thousands of students chanting slogans in favor of independence and democracy. The students lifted up one of their colleagues, Mohamed Abdel Magid Mursi, from the faculty of agriculture, and he was holding high an Egyptian flag when English troops opened fire on him and killed him. As soon as the Egyptian flag fell to the ground another student, Mohamed Abdel Hakam al-Garahi, from the faculty of humanities, rushed to pick it up. An English officer threatened to kill Abdel Hakam if he took a step forward but Abdel Hakam walked on, carrying the flag. The officer fired at him and hit him in the chest. He was taken to hospital, where he breathed his last. All Egypt turned out to say farewell to the martyr, who preferred death to seeing the Egyptian flag fall to the ground. On the first day of the war of October 1973, dozens of Egyptian soldiers gave their lives so that the Egyptian soldier, Mohamed Efendi, could plant the Egyptian flag in Sinai for the first time since it was occupied. So the flag is not just a piece of cloth but a symbol of the nation, of honor and dignity. I thought about that when I saw my country's flag trampled underfoot by the Algerian thugs in Sudan, with some of them taking pleasure in throwing it under cars, driving over it, tearing it up, and burning it. The brutal attacks on Egyptians in Khartoum revealed several facts:

First, it's common at soccer matches for fights to break out between the supporters, but what happened in Khartoum went way beyond fights over soccer. Algerian air force planes had brought thousands of armed Algerian thugs to Khartoum with a specific assignment: to attack and insult Egyptians. The testimony of the victims all indicates that the purpose of the attack was to humiliate Egyptians. What else could it mean when Algerians took off their underwear in front of Egyptian women and chanted in unison, "We're going to screw Egypt"? What was their purpose in forcing Egyptian men to lie down on the ground even after assaulting them with knives and swords? What was their purpose in carrying banners reading "Egypt is the mother of whoredom"? Does this despicable behavior have anything to do with soccer? This rabble cannot represent the great Algerian people who fought with us in the war of October 1973 and whose martyrs shed their blood alongside ours. So why this insistence on humiliating Egyptians when the Algerians had won the match? I would understand it if this was the work of an army of foreign occupation, but it is truly saddening that it should be the work of Arabs. Would any Algerian allow his sister or his mother to be subjected to this kind of intimidation and outrage? The sight of the Egyptian victims weeping on television at the indignity and humiliation cannot be erased from the memory of Egyptians until we bring to account those responsible for this criminal assault.

Second, Egypt is the biggest Arab country and the greatest source of human talent in the Arab world. It was Egyptians who brought about the renaissance in many Arab countries. The universities were set up by Egyptian professors and the newspapers were set up by Egyptian journalists. The institutes of art, cinema, and theater were set up by Egyptian artists. The cities and houses were built by Egyptian architects, the hospitals were established by Egyptian doctors, and even the laws and constitutions there were mostly drawn up by Egyptian law professors. The Algerian national anthem itself was composed by the Egyptian composer, Mohamed Fawzi. Egyptians' special status has made the relationship between Egyptians and other Arab peoples a composite, including love and admiration most of the time and sometimes some touchiness and tension. During the period when Nasserist Arab nationalism was on the rise, Egypt supported the Algerian revolution with money and weapons and defended it at international forums. Egypt also sent its army to support the Yemeni revolution and went to war to defend Palestine and Syria. At that time the feelings of the Arabs toward Egypt were of pure love, but as soon as Egypt stopped performing its pan-Arab mission and signed the Camp David agreements with Israel, all the resentments against Egypt came to the surface.

I do not have space here to enumerate the dozens of examples of the constant attempts by some Arabs to humiliate Egyptians and denigrate their role and their influence, from the way Egyptians in the Gulf have been subjected to the slavery of the 'sponsorship' system, mistreated, and denied their rights; to the way big production companies have often been set up specifically to exclude or marginalize Egyptian talent; and finally to the cultural competitions and festivals held annually at a cost of millions of dollars merely to prove that Egypt is no longer at the forefront of culture and art. All of these are of course desperate, abortive, and ineffective endeavors, first because despite Egypt's difficult circumstances these petty people cannot detract from Egypt's status, and second because Egyptians, an Arab people, cannot deny their Arab identity or dissociate themselves from their Arab brothers, whatever the circumstances.

Third, the Egyptian regime's cooperation with Israel—providing it with gas and cement and taking part in the blockade of Palestinians by closing the Rafah border crossing—are mistaken and dishonorable policies unacceptable first and foremost to Egyptians, who have demonstrated daily in solidarity with their brothers in Iraq, Palestine, and Lebanon. In fact many Egyptians have paid a high price for their Arab nationalist attitudes. Most recently well-known journalist Magdy Ahmed Hussein, who traveled to Gaza in solidarity with the Palestinians under blockade there, was arrested by the Egyptian authorities and sentenced to two years in jail by a military court. The Egyptian regime's position toward Israel does not at all represent the position of the Egyptian people and cannot be used as a pretext to attack and insult Egyptians.

Fourth, the attack on Egyptians in Khartoum was a form of state terrorism in which the Algerian regime was implicated, abetted by the negligence and corruption of the Egyptian regime and its inability to protect Egyptians. A whole week passed after the crime was committed without the Egyptian regime taking a firm and decisive position. Those who expect President Mubarak to restore the lost dignity of Egyptians will have a long wait. What has President Mubarak done for the hundreds of Egyptians detained in Saudi Arabia? What has he done for the Egyptian doctors sentenced to be flogged there? What has he done for the Egyptians tortured in Kuwait? What has President Mubarak done for the Egyptian soldiers killed by Israel on the border, or for the families of the Egyptians whom Israel admits it massacred in war? The answer is always: nothing. Egyptians have lost their rights at home and abroad. Why did the Egyptian authorities allow the Algerian player, Lakhdar Belloumi, to escape after he committed a horrendous crime in Cairo, seriously injuring an innocent Egyptian doctor? Would Belloumi have been allowed to escape if he had committed the crime in a respectable democratic country? Would the series of Algerian attacks on Egyptians have continued if Belloumi had been arrested in Egypt and put on trial?

The rights of citizens are enforced only in a democratic system. The only concern of despotic regimes is to retain power by any means and at any price. The ruler who usurps power, oppresses his people, and falsifies the will of the people at election time cannot convince anyone when he talks about the dignity of citizens. The crime of insulting and humiliating Egyptians in this disgusting way cannot be allowed to pass without question or punishment. If the Egyptian regime is unable to hold the criminals to account, it is the duty of us all as Egyptians to put pressure by all means available on the Algerian regime until it makes an official apology to the Egyptian people and arrests the Algerians who attacked Egyptians and puts them on trial. We should never repay one offense with another and we should not confuse the great Algerian people with the despotic Algerian regime responsible for this crime. But the time has come for everyone to understand that from now on attacking Egyptians will not be easy or without consequences, not at all. Insisting that those who offended our dignity be punished in no way contradicts our pan-Arab commitment, because good stories, as the French proverb says, always make for good friends, and fraternal relations between the Algerian and Egyptian peoples can come about only through respect for the rights of all Egyptians and Algerians.

Democracy is the solution.

November 22, 2009

The Importance of Being Human

I magine you're a westerner from Sweden, France, or the United States. Would you rather spend Christmas and New Year's Eve at home or would you like to spend it lying on the asphalt in the streets of Cairo? The first option is the natural choice because every human being likes to spend the holidays in comfort and respect with his family. But the second option is what fourteen hundred peace-loving foreign activists from forty-two different countries around the world chose to do. They came to Egypt to declare their full solidarity with the Palestinians under blockade in Gaza, bringing them all the food and medicine they could carry. At first the Egyptian authorities agreed to allow the activists in, but when they arrived in Cairo the authorities suddenly decided to stop them from going to Gaza. When the activists protested, the government tried to distract them by offering them free tourist trips. The activists turned these down and insisted on sending the food and medicine to the Palestinians. At that point the Egyptian police attacked them, dragged them along the ground, and beat them brutally. These unfortunate events are significant in more than one way.

First, these foreign activists are intellectuals, writers, artists, and professionals. Each one of them enjoys a dignified life in his or her own country, and some have reached old age, a stage of life when they need rest. But they all share an active humanitarian conscience that makes them refuse to stand by and watch the intentional starvation of a million and a half Palestinians in Gaza. The Israelis' tight blockade has lasted more than two years, having been set up after a massacre in which Israel used internationally prohibited weapons to kill fourteen hundred people, most of them civilians. These chivalrous people who came from their countries to defend the rights of our people in Palestine are merely a sample of those in the West who love peace and justice. They are the people who demonstrate against racism, the brutality of capitalism, globalization policies, and the destruction of the environment by big industrial companies. They are the ones who came out in their millions to protest against the U.S. attack on Iraq. Even if they have not yet succeeded in influencing the decision makers in their governments, they are part of a broad movement that is growing in strength and popularity day by day.

Second, the lesson these activists teach is that our primary duty is to defend the oppressed anywhere and that our sense of being part of humanity takes precedence over any other affiliation. The question here is: Do any of us feel primarily Muslim, Christian, or Arab, or do we consider ourselves to be humans before anything else? The true answer is not contradictory because all religions aim to defend the major human values—justice, truth, and freedom—but the moment we consider ourselves superior to others on grounds of religion or race we quickly descend into hatred and chauvinism. In the same week that these foreigners arrived with aid for the children of Gaza, extremists in Egypt made several deplorable statements warning Egyptian Muslims not to join their Christian compatriots in Christmas celebrations. This illustrates two incompatible views of the world, one tolerant, defending the rights of all humanity without discrimination, and the other extremist, hating and despising those who are different and refusing to recognize their rights. Most of those foreign activists were Christians, and some Jews, but they strongly opposed Israel's criminal policies. An eighty-five-year-old woman in a wheelchair by the name of Hedy Epstein was among them—a survivor of the Nazi Holocaust. In spite of her old age and her deteriorating health she insisted on herself carrying food and gifts for the children of Gaza. Perhaps this noble example of human solidarity should make us pause before we are carried away by the extremist idea that all Christians and Jews, without exception, are the enemies of Islam and of Muslims.

Third, the brutal attack on these activists by some Egyptian policemen was filmed by dozens of cameras and can now be seen across the world on the Internet. I myself saw a video recording in which an Egyptian officer is seen pulling a European woman along the ground by the hair, then beating and kicking her with his fists and his feet. In this way the Egyptian regime proves that it will no longer hesitate to commit any crime in order to please Israel so that Israel puts pressure on the U.S. administration to accept President Mubarak's son, Gamal, as his successor. The Egyptian media is still repeating lies to justify the crime of the steel wall along the border with Gaza, a wall that will eliminate the Palestinians' last chance of getting food and medicine. Every day sycophants from the ruling National Democratic Party come out and tell us that the steel wall is essential and that the tunnels between Egypt and Gaza are used to smuggle drugs and Russian prostitutes (!). This pathetic line no longer convinces anyone. The reputation of the Egyptian regime, in the Arab world and internationally, has never been worse than it is now. The phrase "the Egyptian government's connivance with Israel in the blockade of Gaza" now rings loud in the international media, and the attack on the foreign activists shows that Arab governments are completely in the grip of Zionist influence. If these foreigners who were dragged along the ground and beaten in Cairo had been assaulted in any way under normal circumstances, their embassies would have sent representatives and lawyers immediately and would have done everything they could to assert their rights. But this time they were engaged in overtly anti-Israeli activities and so their embassies in Cairo kept their silence. In fact, western governments, which make such an outcry when demonstrators are suppressed in China or Iran (or in any country that adopts anti-western policies), did not utter a single word as their citizens were dragged along the streets of Cairo, for the simple reason that the activists were protesting against Israel, which no western politician can upset with impunity.

Lastly, the embarrassing question remains. If these foreigners have traveled thousands of miles and left their comfortable lives behind in order to save the children of Gaza from the blockade, what have we Egyptians done? It is true that all Egyptians fully sympathize with our brethren in Gaza, but the reaction in the streets of Egypt falls far short of what it should be. Why don't millions of Egyptians go out on the streets to press the regime to break the blockade of Gaza? There are several reasons, and the first is oppression. In democratic countries people have the right to demonstrate to express their opinions. Demonstrations there receive police protection. But in Egypt, a country ravaged by despotism, anyone who demonstrates is liable to detention, beatings, and torture by State Security.

Another factor is that many leading opinion makers in Egypt are in connivance with the government or afraid to upset it. So when the foreign activists were being beaten by riot police and shouting "Freedom for Gaza," Egyptian opposition parties kept a telling silence and the Muslim Brotherhood confined itself to condemning the wall in parliament without organizing a single protest in the street. It seems that for the Muslim Brotherhood, organizing a demonstration is an extremely difficult operation subject to complex considerations that no one can any longer understand. Egyptians have been surprised by official rulings that building the steel wall to strangle the Palestinians is legitimate under Islamic law coming from members of the Islamic Research Institute, the grand sheikh of al-Azhar, the mufti of the republic, and the minister of religious endowments. As for the sheikhs of the Salafist groups, they have expressed full solidarity with the people of Gaza but strictly forbidden their followers to demonstrate. They say that demonstrations would be of no use because they would not change anything, and because they would include women not wearing the *hijab*. This defeatist logic, with its confused priorities, explains why the Egyptian regime is always lenient toward the Salafist sheikhs, who are always so strict about the details of worship and physical appearance but know their limits well in political matters. Egyptians, like the Palestinians, are completely surrounded by a steel wall of despotism, injustice, and repression, a wall that is strangling them and depriving them of their most basic human rights. The wall is the same, the distress is the same, and the deliverance is also the same.

Democracy is the solution.

January 5, 2010

Who Killed the Egyptians on
the Religious Holiday?

In 1923 a committee was formed to draw up the first Egyptian constitution, but the Wafd (the majority political party at the time) announced it would boycott the committee because it had been set up by appointment rather than through free elections. The committee nonetheless included some of the best minds in Egypt and witnessed an elevated political and intellectual debate about the articles proposed for the Egyptian constitution. Some people argued vociferously in favor of proportional representation for the Copts, so that Copts would always have a certain percentage of the seats in parliament and on local councils. This proposal soon became a major national issue. Those who favored proportional representation wanted fair treatment for the Copts and hoped to avert the possibility of British intervention in Egypt on the pretext of protecting minorities. Those who opposed it refused to view the Copts as a religious minority rather than as Egyptian citizens who should be judged solely by their ability.

The surprising thing is that most of those who opposed proportional representation were Copts. Besides Dr. Taha Hussein, a Muslim, the opponents included Salama Mousa, the intellectual, Professor Aziz Merhom, who collected the signatures of five thousand Copts opposed to the proposal, Father Boutrus Abdel Malik, the chairman of the Church's General Congregational Council, and the head of the Coptic Orthodox Church and many other Copts. In the end the proposal was defeated and Copts won one of the greatest battles in our modern history by refusing to accept sectarian privileges under any guise. I recalled that battle when I was reading about the horrific Nag' Hammadi massacre in which seven Copts were shot dead as they were coming out of church at Coptic Christmas. The question is: Why, seventy years ago, did Copts refuse to accept any sectarian privileges and why are they now being massacred on Christmas Day at church doors? In my opinion these are some of the reasons for the crisis:

First, Egyptian history shows that sectarian strife spreads during times of national frustration. At the beginning of the twentieth century Egyptians went through a phase of despair because of the British occupation and this soon turned into a shameful bout of sectarian conflict (British fingers meddled, as usual), which reached its peak between 1908 and 1911. But as soon as the 1919 uprising happened, everyone united behind it. In fact some Copts, such as Father Sergius, had been advocates of conflict but at the time of the uprising became the fiercest defenders of national unity. There is plenty of frustration, repression, poverty, and injustice in Egypt now, and all these factors push Egyptians toward sectarian hostility, just as they push Egyptians toward violence, crime, and sexual harassment.

Second, in 1923, when Copts rejected sectarian privileges, despite the British occupation Egypt was fighting to set up a democratic secular state in which all citizens would be equal before the law. There was a tolerant Egyptian reading of Islam, the foundations of which were laid by the reformist imam, Mohamed Abduh (1849–1905), who was able to liberate the minds of Egyptians from superstition and extremism. Egypt witnessed a true renaissance in all spheres of activity, such as education for women, theater, cinema, and literature. But since the end of the 1970s, Egypt has come to know another understanding of Islam: the extreme Salafist Wahhabi ideology that Egyptian jurists have termed "the law of the Bedouin." Several factors contributed to the spread of the Wahhabi ideology, primarily the rise in oil prices after the 1973 war, which gave Salafist organizations unprecedented financial resources that they used to propagate their ideas in Egypt and the rest of the world. Then millions of Egyptians went to work in the Gulf states and came back years later steeped in Wahhabi ideas. This ideology also spread under the proven sponsorship of Egyptian state security agencies, which always treated Salafist sheikhs with great tolerance—the opposite of the severe repression to which they subject the Muslim Brotherhood. The reason for this is that Salafist Wahhabism helps to underpin despotic government, as it urges Muslims to obey the ruler and forbids rebellion against him as long as he remains Muslim. The problem is that Wahhabi ideas convey a vision that is hostile to civilization in the true sense of the word, because if they prevailed, art would be *haram*, along with music, singing, cinema, theater, and literature, too. The Wahhabi ideology imposes on women seclusion behind the face-veil or the Turkish burka, which Egyptian women threw off a hundred years ago. It states clearly that democracy is *haram* because it means government by the people while the Wahhabis want to apply God's law (in the way they want, of course).

The gravest aspect of the Salafist Wahhabi ideology is that it completely undermines the concept of citizenship. In Wahhabis' eyes, Copts are not citizens but *dhimmi*s (protected non-Muslims), a defeated and subordinate minority in a country conquered by Muslims. They are also seen as infidels and polytheists prone to hating Islam and conspiring against it. It is forbidden to celebrate their religious holidays or help them build churches because these are not places of worship but places where polytheism is practiced. In the view of the Wahhabis, Christians cannot hold office or lead armies, which implies that they have no loyalty to the nation. Anyone who follows the portrayal of Copts on dozens of satellite channels and Salafist websites is bound to be saddened. These forums, followed by millions of Egyptians daily, openly declare their hatred of Copts and contempt for them. Often they call on Muslims to boycott them. There are countless examples, but I will cite here what I read on the well-known Salafist website, "Guardians of the Faith," which devoted a whole article to the subject, "Why Muslims Are Superior to Copts." "Being a Muslim girl whose role models are the wives of the Prophet, who were required to wear the *hijab*, is better than being a Christian girl, whose role models are whores," it says. "Being a Muslim who fights to defend his honor and his faith is better than being a Christian who steals, rapes, and kills children," it adds. "Being a Muslim whose role models are Muhammad and his companions is better than being a Christian whose role models are Paul the Liar and the whoremongering prophets." As this enmity toward Copts spreads, is it not natural, even inevitable, that it should end in attacks on them?

Third, the virus of extremism has spread from Muslims to Copts, generations of whom have grown up in isolation from society, and some Copts are implicated in the same discourse of extremism and hatred. The best-known is Father Zakaria Boutros, who is dedicated to contesting Islam and insulting Muslims (I have no doubt the Church could silence him immediately if it wanted to). The Church has undertaken to protect the Copts but it has made them more isolated and has changed from being a spiritual authority into being a political party that negotiates in the name of the Coptic people (think about the significance of that expression). Out of fear at the rise of the Muslim Brotherhood the Church has announced, though its senior officials, that it fully accepts the idea of President Mubarak passing on the presidency to his son, Gamal. This attitude, besides being incompatible with the great patriotic record of the Church, does the greatest damage to the Copts because it gives the impression that they are working for the Egyptian regime against the rest of the Egyptians. Similarly, some diaspora Copts have apparently learned none of the lessons of history and have decided to throw all their weight behind foreign powers that have never wanted good for Egypt and that have always raised the slogan of protecting minorities as a pretext for their colonial ambitions. Diaspora Copts have demands, most of which are just, but unfortunately they are completely sectarian, in the sense that they want to solve Copts' problems in isolation from the problems of the nation. Diaspora Copts today are doing the opposite of what their illustrious ancestors did when they rejected proportional representation in 1923. They are not demanding justice and freedom for all Egyptians but insist on obtaining sectarian privileges for themselves alone, as though they were telling the Egyptian regime: "Give us Copts the privileges we demand, then do what you want with other Egyptians. That's none of our business."

There's only one way to see the horrific massacre at Nag' Hammadi: Egyptian citizens were killed on a religious holiday as they were coming out from prayers. The innocents who were killed as they exchanged holiday greetings were Egyptians like me and you. They lived with us, fought alongside us, and defended the country with their blood. They were Egyptians who speak, think, and dream, just like us. They are us, and those who killed them are not those who pulled the triggers. What killed them was a corrupt and despotic regime that subjugates Egyptians, plunders their wealth, and drives them to despair, extremism, and violence.

Democracy is the solution.

January 11, 2010

Can President Obama Save the Copts?

The United States Commission on International Religious Freedom is visiting Egypt this week. The commission consists of nine members, all of them prominent figures in the defense of freedoms. The U.S. president chooses three members, congressional leaders from the ruling party choose two members, and leaders from the other party choose the remaining four. The mandate of this commission is to monitor freedom of religion, thought, and belief, as stipulated in the Universal Declaration of Human Rights. It does not impose sanctions on countries that violate public freedoms but it does issue recommendations that are supposed to be taken into account in formulating U.S. foreign policy. According to newspaper reports, the commission's visit to Cairo had already been organized but it takes on special importance now, in the aftermath of the horrendous Nag' Hammadi massacre in which six innocent Copts and a Muslim policeman were killed at random as they were coming out of church on Christmas Eve. In fact the commission's visit at this time raises more than one issue.

First, any investigation or inquiry by a government commission from another country is a flagrant violation of the sovereignty of the country where the inquiry takes place. Egypt, at least officially, is not a U.S. state or possession, so the commission cannot grant itself the authority to investigate in Egypt. We wonder what would happen if the Egyptian parliament set up a commission to investigate the war crimes U.S. troops commit in Iraq, Afghanistan, and Guantánamo. Would the U.S. administration agree to receive the Egyptian commission and allow it to carry out its inquiry? Unfortunately the answer is obvious. The sad thing is that the Egyptian government plays the national sovereignty card selectively and tendentiously. When Egyptians call for independent international election observers so that elections are not rigged in the usual manner, the Egyptian government forcefully rejects the idea on the grounds of national sovereignty. When the Egyptian government joins Israel in besieging one and half million people in Gaza and the people under siege try to cross into Egypt to save their lives by buying basic needs, the Egyptian government blocks them and orders troops to open fire on them, again on the grounds of national sovereignty. Then Foreign Minister Aboul Gheit shouts out, "If a Palestinian crosses the border, I'll break his leg." But in the case of the U.S. freedoms commissioners, who are now touring Egypt freely from north to south and making inquiries into Egyptian affairs, neither Aboul Gheit nor anyone else can say a single word objecting to their presence.

Second, the purported objectives of this commission are fine and noble but, as always happens with U.S. foreign policy, there is a vast gap between the mission statement and its implementation. The president of the commission, Felice Gaer, is one of the biggest and most prominent supporters of Israel in the United States and has a long history of defending Zionism, to the extent that she has accused international organizations, including the United Nations, of pursuing unjust and biased policies against Israel. I really cannot understand how Ms. Gaer can reconcile her defense of human rights with her defense of Israeli policies. What does she think of burning children with phosphorus, cluster, and napalm bombs? Israel has committed such crimes continuously, starting with the Bahr al-Baqar massacre in Egypt, the Qana massacre, and to the recent massacre in Gaza. Does Ms. Gaer think that burning the skin of Arab children with internationally prohibited weapons is compatible with the principles of the human rights she defends in her commission?

Third, if the commission is interested in the persecution of Copts in Egypt, we ask whether the commissioners are interested in Copts in defense of human rights or because Copts are Christians. If it is in defense of human rights, then we would remind you that tens of thousands of young Islamists in Egypt have been living for years in the dark depths of detention camps without trial or charge, and many of them have received several court rulings in favor of their release, which the Egyptian government has not carried out and never will. Why doesn't the commission defend the right of these detainees to justice and freedom? Do they not have the same human rights as the Copts? And what does the commission think of the crimes—rape, killing of civilians, and torture—attributed to U.S. soldiers in Iraq? Has it had time to investigate these crimes? I advise the freedoms commission to travel immediately from Cairo to Nigeria, where reports say sectarian massacres have led to the deaths of dozens of innocent people, mainly Muslims. Here I will cite a report by a respected impartial international organization, Human Rights Watch, which says:

> Groups of armed men attacked the largely Muslim population of Kuru Karama around 10 a.m. on January 19, 2010. After surrounding the town, they hunted down and attacked Muslim residents, some of whom had sought refuge in homes and a local mosque, killing many as they tried to flee and burning many others alive.

What does the distinguished commission think of this massacre? Is it compatible with human rights?

Fourth, can one take a fragmentary approach to defending human rights? Can one defend only the rights of Christians in a country governed by a despotic regime through an emergency law, rigging elections, repression, and detention camps? The answer is obvious. Human rights are never divisible, but U.S. foreign policy as usual is contradictory and hypocritical. The U.S. administration, in order to protect its interests and the interests of Israel, provides complete backing to the worst despotic rulers in the Arab world and turns a blind eye to the crimes they commit against their own people, but at the same time it sends commissions to investigate the persecution of Copts.

Fifth, what happened on Christmas Eve in Nag' Hammadi was a horrendous sectarian massacre that shook all of Egypt, and Copts have a right to be angry and to demand everything that would prevent its repetition. But they have to remember two things. First, the Egyptian regime that has failed to protect Copts is the same regime the Coptic Church supports with all its strength, to the extent that Pope Shenouda and senior church leaders have clearly announced more than once that they would welcome President Mubarak passing on the presidency of Egypt to his son, Gamal (as though Egypt were a poultry farm). Second, it is natural and legitimate that Copts inside Egypt and abroad should protest against the massacre, but to call in western countries and ask them to intervene is unacceptable conduct that could push Coptic anger beyond its legitimate limits. I do not believe that the conscience of any Egyptian patriot, whether Muslim or Christian, would allow him or her to invite foreign powers to intervene in Egypt, however grave the injustices Egyptians suffer and however much they oppose the regime in power. Egyptians are all persecuted. Millions of poor people in Egypt are deprived of freedom, justice, dignity, and the rights to work, housing, and healthcare. It is true that the Copts suffer a double injustice, once as Egyptians and again as Copts, but the legitimate demands of Copts cannot be met separately from the demands of the nation. We cannot demand justice for Copts alone, excluding other Egyptians. Those Copts who seek protection through foreign powers are committing a serious mistake that will tarnish the image of all Copts and suggest that they are agents of foreign powers. However much some Copts seek the help of President Obama or other western leaders, they will never obtain their rights through foreign intervention, because what governs western policy is interests rather than principles, and the history of western states is replete with examples of total political iniquity. One might recall the shah of Iran, who lived his whole life as a servant to the interests of the United States, yet the U.S. abandoned him in one day and left him alone to face his destiny in the deluge of the Iranian revolution.

The demands of the Copts must be national, not sectarian. The proper place for the Copts is not at all in the corridors of western foreign ministries. Their proper place is here, in Egypt, with their Egyptian brothers, fighting for justice and freedom. When the despotic regime disappears and all Egyptians wrest back their natural right to choose their rulers freely, when emergency law, election rigging, repression, and torture come to an end, only then will all Egyptians, Muslims and Copts, obtain the rights they have been denied.

Democracy is the solution.

January 25, 2010

Egypt Awakened

Although the Egyptian government officially ignored the arrival of
Mohamed ElBaradei in Egypt, it did in fact send a clear message
to Egyptians when the Interior Ministry detained several young
people simply for urging Egyptians to go out and welcome him. The security agencies also made it clear that they would not allow Egyptians to
rally to greet ElBaradei at the airport and announced they had mobilized
eight thousand riot police to deal with anyone who gathered there. These
unofficial statements were leaked and some 'independent' newspapers
published them on their front pages in the same form on the morning
ElBaradei arrived in Egypt. I read these reports as I was preparing to go
to the airport and I was certain that, given this campaign of intimidation,
Egyptians would naturally be reluctant to go and welcome ElBaradei. It's
true that greeting someone at the airport can never amount to a crime,
even under the emergency law by which President Mubarak has governed
Egypt for the past thirty years, but since when have the Egyptian police
needed a charge to arrest anyone they want? Egyptian citizens know well
the extent of the abuses committed by the security agencies. On many previous occasions the security agencies have not flinched from committing
horrendous crimes to suppress demonstrators: beatings, detention, sexual
abuse of protesters, and hiring thugs and calling in convicted criminals
to shed protesters' blood while policemen look on without intervening.
I knew that, and I told myself that although it is true that Egyptians like
and support ElBaradei, it is also true that fear is a human instinct we have
to understand. I braced myself not to be disappointed if only a meager
number turned out. But as soon as I reached the airport I was taken by
surprise by hundreds of Egyptians, who soon became thousands, all of

whom had come to greet ElBaradei. They were not frightened by the government's terrorism or the threats of the security agencies. They wanted to prove to the whole world that they would support Mohamed ElBaradei and would work with him to recover the rights they have lost. The vast and impressive popular reception that Egyptians organized for Mohamed ElBaradei's return to Egypt conveys several important messages:

First, from now on no one can accuse Egyptians of being passive, submissive to injustice, disengaged from public affairs, or any other of those claims that no longer reflect the reality of Egypt. The thousands of Egyptians who conquered their fear and gathered at the airport to welcome ElBaradei were not professional politicians, and most of them did not belong to political parties. They were very ordinary Egyptians, like our neighbors or our colleagues at work, and they came from different provinces and different social classes. Some of them came in luxury cars and many came by public transport. They included university professors, professionals, students, farmers, writers, artists, and housewives, Muslims and Copts, women with and without veils and some wearing *niqab*. These Egyptians, different in every way, all agreed on change, on serious work to restore justice and freedom. Egyptian public opinion, once a hypothetical term, has now become a real popular force whose influence is growing day by day. That force revealed itself in all its strength on the day of the reception for ElBaradei.

Second, I congratulate Dr. Mohamed ElBaradei on the trust Egyptians have in him at the same time as I realize the weight of the responsibility thrown on his shoulders. The thousands of Egyptians who stood all day to greet him are in fact representative of the millions of Egyptians who like him and trust him. I was standing in the middle of the crowd when an old woman came up to me and asked to speak to me in private. I took her aside and in a low voice she asked me, "Do you think the government will do anything to harm Dr. ElBaradei?" When I assured her that this was most unlikely, she sighed with relief and said, "May God protect him." For millions of Egyptians Mohamed ElBaradei has become a symbol of hope for change in every sense. Perhaps the deafening chants at the airport—"Here are the crowds, ElBaradei; there's no going back, ElBaradei"—clearly reflect how much Egyptians trust ElBaradei and that they are confident, as I am, that he will never let them down.

Third, the truly exhilarating aspect of this reception was the great work done by thousands of young people of both genders, most of them university students or young graduates. These people form the power base of support for Mohamed ElBaradei, the unknown soldiers in organizing this historic reception. They set up Facebook groups to support ElBaradei, some of which attracted seventy thousand members, and they prepared well for the reception, using their technical expertise to set up an extensive and effective communications network on the Internet. Several days in advance they prepared and distributed everything necessary: maps of the airport and specific instructions on how to get there by public transport or by car. They even drew up an emergency plan in case the police prevented them from entering and set up a dedicated hot line for people to call if they were detained. The names of the organizers should be recorded on a roll of honor: poet Abdel Rahman Youssef, Heba Elwa, Ahmed Maher, Amr Ali, Bassem Fathi, Nasser Abdel Hamid, Abdel Moneim Imam, and dozens of their colleagues, who really set a high standard for bravery and orderly and systematic national action.

Fourth, from the start the security forces decided not to block people because the international media were all present at the airport and would have caused a major scandal, which the regime did not want, if security had attacked ordinary citizens who had come to greet a respectable public figure who is well-known internationally. Another reason is that the security agencies were confident that Egyptians would be frightened off by the threats and the detentions and that the number of people at the airport would be insignificant. The security agencies did not interfere with the people already inside the airport, but when the number had grown to several thousand, police officers began to harass people just arriving. They kept out all those carrying banners in support of ElBaradei and anyone they suspected was coming to greet him. When ElBaradei's plane landed, the arrival hall was chock full of people chanting slogans and singing songs. But security prevented ElBaradei from coming out, and closed the gate on the pretext of maintaining his safety. The fact is that security could easily have protected ElBaradei but the decision to keep him back was basically political, because to have ElBaradei emerge surrounded by thousands of chanting supporters in front of the western media was more than the regime could tolerate. Security officials took ElBaradei out through another gate, far from his supporters, but he sent them a message through his brother, Dr. Ali ElBaradei, saying he would come to greet them. The thousands stood around waiting until ElBaradei's car appeared and he saw for himself the people's genuine enthusiasm for him.

Friday was a wonderful day in my life because I truly felt I belonged to a great nation. I will always remember the atmosphere of sincerity and enthusiasm I experienced. I will not forget the sight of the thousands of people chanting "Long live Egypt" or singing the national anthem. Some of them could not control their feelings and wept. I will not forget the people eagerly discussing what ElBaradei should do now that he is back in Egypt. They were speaking with the affection and intimacy of friends, though they were meeting for the first time. I will not forget the man who came with his wife and their pretty little girl with two plaits, who sat on his shoulders carrying a picture of ElBaradei. I will not forget the people who gave out mineral water and cold drinks to those present. I will not forget the dignified woman in the *hijab*, the good-hearted Egyptian mother who brought with her several packets of fine dates. She opened them one after the other and started to give them out to people standing around that she did not know. When someone said, "No, thank you," she gave them an angry look, then smiled and said, "You must eat something. You've been on your feet all day and you must be hungry. Please have some."

This is the Egypt that has woken up, an Egypt that from today onward no one can enslave, treat with contempt, or oppress.

Democracy is the solution.

February 21, 2010

The Story of Mamdouh Hamza

D r. Mamdouh Hamza is one of the best civil engineers in Egypt.
He has supervised dozens of major projects in Egypt and around
the world, including in the United States, Britain, and Japan. He
has received countless prestigious international prizes and his achievements are a real source of pride for Egyptians and all Arabs. Aside from
his professional distinction, Dr. Hamza has a deep sense of public service
and believes that knowledge brings with it a responsibility to mankind.
He often says that since poor Egyptian taxpayers covered the costs of
his studies at Cairo University he has a duty to use his knowledge to help
them as much as he can.

When floods recently hit Aswan Province and made thousands of
people homeless, Dr. Hamza felt he should do something for the victims,
so he appeared on the Orbit television channel with presenter Amr al-
Dib and volunteered to help build alternative housing for those displaced
by the floods. Donations poured in to the program and soon reached 28
million Egyptian pounds (about $5 million), which was deposited in the
account of a charitable organization for the housing project. Enthusiastic
about the project, Dr. Hamza abandoned his private work in Cairo and
traveled to Aswan to supervise the building work in person for free. As one
would expect, the governor of Aswan, Major General Mustafa al-Sayed,
welcomed Dr. Hamza warmly and thanked him for contributing his time
and effort for the sake of the poor. The governor quickly had a piece of
land set aside for the project but then instead offered another piece that
was rocky and difficult to build on. But Dr. Hamza, who is a professor of
soil mechanics and foundation engineering, accepted the challenge and
managed to overcome the problem of the rugged terrain, building twenty-

nine houses in the record time of three weeks. Because of his experience he was also able to keep the costs down to the unprecedented amount of 35,000 pounds (about $7,000) per house. Dr. Hamza hoped to extend his project to other parts of Egypt in order to provide shelter for millions of Egyptians who live in inhumane conditions in shantytowns, without basic services such as electricity and sewage systems.

Work was proceeding rapidly and everything seemed propitious for Dr. Hamza's project to house the poor, but the winds suddenly changed and instead of offering appreciation and praise, the authorities in Aswan turned against Mamdouh Hamza. They refused to provide the project with water, refused to give Dr. Hamza building permits, and refused to pay the wages they had agreed to pay the builders. They even froze the account with the citizen donations and threatened the charity with severe measures if it disbursed a single pound to Dr. Hamza of the donations people had contributed because they trusted his sincerity and competence. They even went as far as to report the project to the police, who arrested some of the engineers and builders while they were working at the site. The police took control of the site, stopped the work, and refused to take statements from Dr. Hamza. In this way Dr. Hamza became enemy number one for the governor of Aswan, who called in some engineers, all of them former students of Dr. Hamza at the college of engineering, to write reports asserting that the houses in the project had construction flaws. Most of the engineers refused to go against their consciences and wrote reports praising the work of their mentor. The governor shelved those reports because they were not to his liking. In the end the governor of Aswan referred the matter to the public prosecutor, a strange procedure given that Dr. Hamza is not a murderer or a thief who requires questioning by prosecutors, but rather a great Egyptian who wanted to serve his country by volunteering his money, time, and effort. Unfortunately we cannot be optimistic about the investigations because the public prosecutor is not independent of the political authorities in Egypt. The question arises: Why did the regime turn against Mamdouh Hamza and oppose him so fiercely after initially welcoming his project? The reasons are as follows:

First, the houses Dr. Hamza built were very inexpensive at 35,000 pounds each, compared with the 80,000 pounds Aswan Province spends on houses for the poor. The difference between the two costs goes into the pockets of big contractors who enjoy close and influential relationships with government agencies. These contractors see the success of Dr. Hamza's project as the basis for a new model for housing the poor. They realize that if it were to spread, it would be a serious threat to their interests because they would lose millions in profits. Hence they would do everything possible to put an end to Dr. Hamza's project.

Second, the projects carried out by the provincial authorities will be inaugurated by Suzanne Mubarak, the wife of President Mubarak, and in the minds of officials it would never do for Mrs. Mubarak to open high-cost housing projects for the poor while Mamdouh Hamza is succeeding in building better houses at half the cost. Perhaps the nightmare that haunts senior officials is that Mrs. Mubarak might hear about Mamdouh Hamza's successful project and ask them this logical question: "How can Dr. Mamdouh Hamza build houses for the poor at half the cost that you charge?"

Third, if Dr. Hamza's project were successful, this would prove his administrative skills and his well-known engineering talent, which might lead to mention of his name as a strong candidate for a ministerial position in any early cabinet reshuffle. This possibility in particular frightens ministers who are trembling with fear for their positions and who consider Dr. Hamza and anyone of similar competence to be dangerous rivals who might replace them.

Fourth, Mamdouh Hamza's project depended wholly on private donations and was independent of any governmental or quasi-governmental body. It is a successful model that can be repeated across the country. It would create a popular force that would challenge the government and set up projects that are better than those of the state. The Egyptian regime, like all despotic regimes, is not at all comfortable with the idea of an independent popular force, even on a matter such as housing for the poor, because those who rally today to build houses with their own money and effort will definitely one day rally to demand their political rights.

The story of Dr. Mamdouh Hamza, though frustrating, is useful, and I offer it to all those who still believe that a renaissance can come about in our country without political reform. Some generous people still imagine that if every Egyptian worked hard then Egypt would progress without the need for democratic change. But this well-intentioned idea is in fact extremely naïve because it assumes that the effect of despotism is limited to parliament and the government. The truth is that despotism, like a cancer, starts in the political system and spreads rapidly through all government agencies, crippling and destroying them. Despotism definitely leads to the corruption of the state, which quickly leads to the formation of malignant gangs inside the regime who amass great fortunes through corruption and are prepared to fight viciously and destroy any person, any idea, and any project to preserve their gains. The added fact that a despotic regime gives priority to loyalty over competence, and therefore gives jobs to loyal supporters who usually are not objectively qualified to do the job, makes them dread the appearance of anyone really competent who might take over their position. That's how a despotic system is transformed into a frightful machine that routinely eliminates people of talent, fighting and persecuting them, while at the same time attracting failures and incompetents as long as they sing and dance for the president and praise his genius and magnificent achievements.

In the end all this leads to a deterioration of the state's performance in every field until the country reaches rock bottom, as has happened in Egypt. What happened to Dr. Hamza is exactly what happened previously to Dr. Ahmed Zewail and all the talented Egyptians who have tried to do something to help their country. All this proves once again that Egypt cannot be saved from its current nightmare by individual efforts, however sincere and enthusiastic. Any attempt at reform without democratic change is simply a waste of time and effort.

Democracy is the solution.

May 10, 2010

Who is Killing the Poor in Egypt?

Mohamed Fathy, a brilliant journalist and a talented writer, recently went on holiday to Alexandria with his two children, his wife, and her sister, Nashwa. They all had a wonderful time and then suddenly an unfortunate incident took place. A speeding car hit Nashwa as she was crossing the road and she suffered serious injuries and fractures, her clothes were torn, and she lost consciousness. Because she was alone at the time of the accident some passersby took her to the government hospital in the center of the city. So far the story would appear normal—a woman is injured in a traffic accident and taken to a hospital for treatment—but what happened after that is beyond imagination. Nashwa and dozens of other injured people were dumped into a place called the Awatef al-Naggar Emergency Unit and she stayed there for two hours without any first aid or treatment and without any doctor examining her. Mohamed Fathy arrived at the hospital and found Nashwa at death's door. He asked for a doctor to examine her but nobody paid any attention. With the passage of time and the apathy of the hospital staff, Fathy lost his temper and started shouting at everyone he met: "We need a doctor, I beg you! The patient is going to die!"

No doctor came up to examine Nashwa, but a policeman came to inform Mohamed Fathy that he was forbidden from staying by her side because she was in a women's ward and no men were allowed there. Fathy began threatening them by saying he was a journalist and he would write a story about all the crimes they commit against poor patients. Only then did a doctor appear to examine Nashwa, a full three hours after she arrived in pieces at the hospital. The doctor then announced that she needed to have some scans. He left it at that and abandoned her where she was. After much effort Mohamed Fathy managed to get in touch with the director of the hospital, Dr. Mohamed al-Maradny, who seemed extremely upset at the idea that anyone might contact him about patients. Sarcastically the doctor asked Fathy, "And what can I do for you, sir?"

Fathy told him that his wife's sister was dying and had been dumped in his hospital without any medical attention or scans for more than three hours. At that point Dr. al-Maradny said, "Delays with scans are quite normal. Even if you're in a private hospital and you pay the doctors' fees, scans can be delayed."

The hospital director was trying to remind Fathy that Nashwa was receiving free treatment so her family did not have the right to complain about anything. Fathy spoke to the director at length about humaneness and the doctor's duty to tend to the sick, and after a long conversation the director (who appears to manage the hospital from afar by telephone) did order immediate scans for Nashwa. At this point a new problem arose. A cleaner came up to Nashwa, whose condition had greatly deteriorated, and was about to carry her in his arms to the scans department. Mohamed Fathy objected, arguing that carrying patients with fractures required a trained medic because moving the patient's body carelessly could cause death. The hospital staff ridiculed Fathy's idea, which seemed very strange to them. "What do you mean, medic? We don't have that kind of thing here. Either this man carries her or we leave her where she is," they said. The cleaner went up to poor Nashwa and shouted, "Come on, let's hope for the best. Lift, lift!" He gave her a violent yank and her screams resounded throughout the hospital.

At last Nashwa had a CAT scan, and then it was the turn of the C-scan operator. This man, by the consensus of the hospital staff, was always sullen and morose, treating patients rudely and arrogantly, and if he did not like a patient he announced that the machine was out of order and declined to do the scan, no matter how serious the patient's condition. On top of that he was bearded and had Salafist ideas. The scan operator was dawdling around in his room and Fathy went to him several times, begging him to come and do the scan for Nashwa. At last the man came and shouted at everyone present, "Women out. I don't want any women here." Fathy's wife tried to explain to him that she was the patient's sister but the man insisted she get out. He allowed Fathy to stay on the grounds that he was *mahram*, sufficiently closely related to Nashwa under Islamic law. He then grabbed Nashwa's arm violently and when she screamed he shouted at her angrily, "Keep your voice right down. I don't want to hear a sound." Mohamed Fathy found himself in a difficult situation. If he argued with the bearded scan operator Nashwa might lose her chance to have the scan and might die. So he resorted to a trick to win the man's approval. He starting talking to Nashwa using Salafist expressions: "Don't forget to put on the headscarf you left outside. Never mind, sister. May God reward you well, sir. Recite the Qur'an. God is the one whose help we seek, sir. May God reward you well, may God reward you well." The stratagem achieved its purpose. The bearded scan operator gave way, approved of the patient, and carried out the scan.

After all this negligence, which was close to criminal, it would have been natural for Nashwa to die in the government hospital, but God wanted to grant her a new life and, almost miraculously, Mohamed Fathy managed to move her to a private hospital where she underwent an emergency operation that saved her life. This incident, full of details I received from Mohamed Fathy, contains the answer to the question, who is killing the poor in Egypt?

Responsibility for the deaths of poor patients in state-run hospitals goes beyond the minister of health to the president of the republic himself. Egypt's tragedy begins with President Mubarak, who, despite our respect for his person and his status, was not elected by anyone and is not accountable to anyone and so feels no real need to win the approval of Egyptians or pay much attention to what they think about what he does. He knows he holds power by force and has a massive apparatus of repression that can punish without mercy anyone who tries to remove him. This president, who is above any oversight and immune against change, chooses and dismisses his ministers for reasons he does not feel compelled to explain to the public, and so these ministers are answerable only to him and not to Egyptians. Their only concern is to please the president; they have no interest at all in what happens to people as a result of their policies. We have only to remember how health minister Hatem al-Gabali, who is responsible for the deaths of hundreds of patients in his wretched hospitals, abandoned everything and stayed for weeks with the president while he was being treated in Germany. As far as the minister of health is concerned, the health of the president is a thousand times more important than the lives of poor people, because only the president has the power to dismiss him at any moment.

In such complete alienation between power and people, we see a model of the Egyptian government. The hospital director manages to win the approval of his superiors in some way and is then immune to any oversight and does not even take the trouble to go to his hospital, instead running it by telephone. He treats poor patients as annoying creatures who are a burden to him and to society. Then there is the warped behavior of the scan operator, who is just as poor, wretched, and frustrated as the patients but whose sense of wretchedness is transformed into hostility toward the patients. He enjoys controlling and humiliating them and at the same time understands religion as appearance, ways of dress, and acts of worship divorced from human values such as honesty and compassion, which are the most important parts of religion. This vicious cycle, which starts with despotism and leads to negligence and corruption, recurs every day in Egypt and ends in the deaths of more poor people. What happened in the government hospital in Alexandria is exactly what has happened with the dozens of buildings that have collapsed on top of inhabitants, the ferries that have sunk, and the trains that have caught fire. It is saddening that the number of people who have died from corruption and negligence in Egypt is greater than the number who have died in all its wars. In other words the Egyptian regime has killed more Egyptians than Israel. The horrendous crimes committed against the poor every day will not stop because a manager is transferred or a worker punished. When the president and his ministers are elected and accountable and can be removed from office by the people, only then will they care for the health, life, and dignity of Egyptians.

Democracy is the solution.

August 12, 2010

Does Subservience Protect Us from Injustice?

The story goes that a peasant laborer acquired a vast fortune and bought a large boat of the kind they call a *dahabiya* in the countryside. He bought smart and expensive clothes and sat in his *dahabiya* as it glided across the water. The man who owned the land he worked on, an arrogant and cruel-hearted man, saw him and ordered his workers to storm the *dahabiya* and arrest the peasant. They brought him before the landowner and the following exchange took place between them:

Landowner: Since when have peasants been sailing new *dahabiya*s?

Peasant: It's all thanks to your compassion, your justice, and your generosity, sir. This should make you happy because it's a sign of your grace and goodness.

Landlord: How can peasants be allowed to imitate their masters and sail *dahabiya*s?

Peasant: God forbid that I should imitate my masters. Who am I? I'm just one of your slaves and everything I earn is your property in the end.

Landlord: If you don't want to imitate us, why did you buy a *dahabiya* and why are you sailing it on the Nile as if you're one of the masters of the country? Do you want the other peasants to see you and think you're someone of importance and standing?

Peasant: God forbid, my lord. If you think I've done anything wrong then I swear by God and His Prophet that I'll never sail this *dahabiya* again. I repent right now, sir. I beg you to accept my repentance.

Landlord: I accept but I'll take steps to make sure you never repeat your mistake.

The landlord gave orders to his servants, who tied the peasant up and dragged him along the ground until his new clothes were covered with mud and ripped to shreds. Then they started to beat him until his knees, his feet, and his back were bleeding. Meanwhile the landlord laughed and said, "That way you'll never forget your humble place, you peasant."

This incident did in fact take place in an Egyptian village early in the twentieth century and is told by the great writer, Ahmed Amin, in his excellent book, *Qamus al-'adat wa-l-taqalid al-misriya* (A Dictionary of Egyptian Customs and Traditions). To my mind it reflects a widespread pattern for the relationship between the despot and his victims. No doubt the peasant knew that he had a right to sail the *dahabiya* because he had bought it with his own money, and that he also had a right to wear whatever clothes he wanted. The peasant knew he had done nothing wrong but he thought it would be wise to apologize to the landowner and repent in public for an offense he had never committed. The peasant was especially servile in order to escape injustice, although if he had stood his ground courageously against the landowner to defend his right to be treated as human being, he would at least have maintained his dignity and the consequences of being courageous would have been no worse than the consequences of being submissive.

I remember this lesson when I follow what is happening in Egypt these days, because generations of Egyptians have grown up in the firm belief that submitting to injustice is the ultimate wisdom and that bowing and scraping to those in power is the best way to protect themselves from harm. Egyptians have long believed that objecting to the authoritarian system is sheer folly and will never change things for the better. They think that those who resist injustice will have their lives destroyed and be detained, tortured, and even killed. Egyptians have believed that coexistence with the authoritarian regime will save them from the harm it can inflict, trusting that the vast apparatus of repression the state possesses only goes into action to crush those who stand in its way, that the regime will never harm those who bow down and obey and who concentrate on making a living and bringing up their children. On the contrary, Egyptians think the regime will protect and look after them. But now, perhaps for the first time in decades, they are waking up to the fact that submission, failing to speak out for justice, and being obsequious toward oppressors will not at all prevent injustice, but often add to it.

Khaled Mohamed Said, the young man who was killed in Alexandria, was no political activist and did not belong to any front or movement that aimed to overthrow the regime. In fact he may never in his life have taken part in any demonstration. He was a completely peaceful young Egyptian, dreaming like millions of Egyptians of escaping by any possible means from his oppressive homeland to a country where he could live in freedom and dignity. He was waiting to obtain a U.S. passport like his brothers so that he could leave Egypt forever. On the evening of his death he went to an Internet café to pass the time, again like millions of others. He committed no crime and broke no law, but as soon as he went into the café two plainclothes policemen pounced on him and without a word started beating him brutally. They banged his head on the edge of the marble table with all their might, dragged him out of the café, and took him into a nearby building, where they continued to beat him and banged his head against the iron gate of the building until their purpose was fulfilled. Khaled's skull was smashed and he died in front of them. Regardless of the real reason behind this brutal murder, and regardless also of the successive statements issued by the Ministry of Interior to justify the crime, all of which have turned out to be untrue, the clear meaning of this murder is that submission is no longer enough to protect Egyptians from repression. Khaled Said was beaten in the same way as young people demonstrating for freedom. There is no difference.

Repression in Egypt no longer distinguishes between demonstrators and people taking part in sit-ins on the one hand and people sitting in cafés and sleeping at home on the other. The murder of Khaled Said in this brutal manner and the fact that the killers have escaped punishment plainly indicate that any police officer, and even any plainclothes detective, can kill whomever he wants and the apparatus of despotism will step in at once to exonerate the killer. They have ample and effective means to do so, thanks to the emergency law and the fact that the judiciary is not independent of the presidency. The millions of Egyptians who wept when they saw the picture of Khaled Said with his skull smashed, his teeth knocked out, and his face mangled from the beating were not weeping only out of sympathy for Khaled and his poor mother. They were also weeping because they imagined that the faces of their children might tomorrow be in the place of Khaled Said's face. The picture of Khaled

Said's military service certificate, published in the newspapers alongside the picture of his mutilated body, reflects the saddening truth: Egypt is now doing to its own people what Egypt's enemies have not done.

Any Egyptian might suffer the same fate as Khaled Said. In fact it has already happened to hundreds of thousands of them: those who drowned on the ferries of death, those buried under collapsed buildings because of building licenses obtained corruptly and substandard building materials, those who died of disease because of rotten foodstuffs imported by big merchants, those who have killed themselves in despair at their future, and the university students who tried to flee the country to clean toilets in Europe but drowned aboard the sinking ships of death. All of these were completely peaceful citizens and it never occurred to them to resist despotism. In fact they believed, just like the peasant in the story, that they could coexist with the regime, bow down before the oppressor, and then set up their own small safe world for themselves and their children, but they all lost their lives because of the regime they were afraid to confront. In other words what happened to them as a result of submitting was exactly what they feared might happen if they protested and rebelled.

The wave of protests sweeping Egypt from one end to the other today is essentially due to the fact that life for millions of poor people, which was already hard, has become impossible. The more important reason for these vehement protests is that Egyptians have realized that silence about justice will not protect them from injustice. For thirty years, Egyptians have tried the individual solution. Egyptians used to escape hell at home by going to the Gulf countries, where they often faced another kind of humiliation and subjugation. After a few years they would come back with enough money to live a comfortable life, far from the general context of Egyptian suffering. These individual solutions no longer work and Egyptians are now under siege in their own country. They have finally learned the lesson the peasant in the story did not understand: that the consequences of courage are never worse than the consequences of fear, and that the only way to escape an oppressive ruler is to confront him with all our strength.

Democracy is the solution.

June 22, 2010

Does Mistreating People Invalidate the Ramadan Fast?

Some years ago I used to take the subway from Sayyida Zeinab every day and in front of the station there were peddlers who would spread their various wares on the sidewalk. One of them was a quiet and courteous old man of more than sixty who always wore a *gallabiya* and an old jacket and offered padlocks, screwdrivers, plastic tablecloths, glasses, and other such simple things. One morning in Ramadan I saw the police carry out a raid on the peddlers to move them off the streets. Most of the peddlers picked up their goods, ran off at top speed, and escaped, but the old man was unable to flee in time. The police confiscated his goods and when he started shouting and calling for help the officer in charge launched into a tirade of vicious insults. When the old man continued to shout, the policemen gave him a vicious beating, arrested him, and took him off. The strange thing was that the faces of the policemen who beat him were pale from the effects of fasting. I thought about the fact that those who mistreated the old peddler never had any doubt that their Ramadan fasting would count from the point of view of Islamic law. I found myself wondering: How can we fast for Ramadan and abuse people at the same time? Isn't abusing people one of the things that invalidate one's fasting?

I referred back to books on Islamic jurisprudence and found that seven things invalidate fasting: eating and drinking; acts similar to eating and drinking; sexual intercourse; masturbation; deliberate vomiting; the cupping of blood; and menstruation and bleeding after childbirth. So all the things that invalidate fasting are related to one's body, even though the Prophet Muhammad said, "He who does not give up uttering falsehood and acting according to it, God has no need of his giving up his food and his drink." Based on this hadith, some jurists have said that some noncorporeal acts can invalidate fasting, such as lying and mistreating or slandering people, but the majority has confined acts that invalidate fasting to physical acts and believes that improper conduct deprives one of the reward for fasting but does not in itself invalidate fasting. So someone who vomits deliberately automatically breaks the fast whereas those who lie, are hypocritical, mistreat people, or deprive them of their rights have not invalidated their fast.

With this strange concept of fasting we find ourselves face to face with a mistaken reading of religion. In many cases rituals have become an end in themselves instead of a means to improve and chasten oneself. The road to piety has become a series of defined and invariable steps as though we were dealing with the process of setting up a commercial company or having a passport issued. For many, Islam has been transformed into a package of measures a Muslim has to complete without this necessarily having any effect on his or her conduct in life. This disconnect between dogma and conduct has coincided with a period of decadence in the Islamic world; in fact it is the primary reason for that decadence. If you want to make sure of that, all you have to do is head to the nearest police station, where you will find people being beaten and humiliated, all by people who are fasting and do not have the slightest doubt about the validity of their fasting. In Egypt there are tens of thousands of Islamist detainees who have spent long years behind bars without trial. Many of them have obtained court orders for their release but the orders have remained mere pieces of paper, unimplemented. Those responsible for wrecking the lives of these wretches and their families are Muslims who are rarely without calluses on their foreheads from regular praying and who never feel that what they are doing makes them any less religious. It is even more amazing to see what happens on security premises where detainees are tortured to extract the required confessions. In these human slaughterhouses, which belong to the darkness of the Middle Ages, there is always a prayer room where the torturers can perform their prayers at the appointed times.

Is anyone more zealous about their religious observance than the leaders of the ruling National Democratic Party, who have rigged elections and plundered, impoverished, and humiliated the Egyptian people? This mistaken understanding of religion is what has turned the month of Ramadan, which was once a divine occasion to set at rights the behavior of mankind, into a massive carnival where we all yell and shout, pray and fast, generally without any impact on the way we deal with other people. When I see thousands of Muslims flocking to mosques every night for special Ramadan prayers I feel a mixture of joy and sadness. I rejoice because I can see that Muslims are committed to their religion and nothing can deter them from fulfilling their religious obligations, and I am sad because these thousands upon thousands of people have missed the true message of Islam, that the ultimate jihad is to speak truth to tyrants. Many Muslims see Islam as just wearing the *hijab* and the full face-veil, praying, and going to Mecca. These people rise up in vociferous protest at the sight of a naked actress and lead violent campaigns to ban beauty pageants, but in the face of despotism and oppression they do not utter a single word. In fact they bow down in submission to the tyrant's injustice, with never a thought of rebellion.

These Muslims, in their deficient understanding of Islam, are the victims of two types of cleric: the government's clerics and the Wahhabi clerics. The government's clerics are civil servants who receive their salaries and perquisites from the government and hence select from Islam everything that supports the wishes of the ruler, however corrupt or oppressive he may be, while the Wahhabi clerics assert that to disobey a Muslim ruler is unlawful even if he is corrupt, and that obeying him is obligatory even if he has stolen from Muslims and has had them whipped unjustly. The Wahhabis distract Muslims with everything that is secondary in religion. In Egypt there are dozens of Wahhabi television channels, financed with oil money, with daily appearances by sheikhs who receive millions of pounds a year for preaching sermons to Egyptians, half of whom live in abject poverty. Sheikhs of this kind appear on screen alongside advertisements for washing machines, refrigerators, creams for removing skin blotches, and depilatory products for women. They preach to Muslims about everything other than what they really need. You will not find a single one of them speaking about torture, election rigging, or unemployment, or warning Egyptians that the ruler might bequeath them to his son like a herd of beasts. Some of these sheikhs have no qualms about cooperating openly and fully with the security services and some of them have ruled that demonstrations and strikes are forbidden to Muslims. In other words, they not only fail to speak out for justice but also assist the ruler in oppression when they prevent people from demanding the restoration of their rights.

This superficial piety, which is the fundamental reason for our back-wardness, was described a hundred years ago by the great reformer, Mohamed Abduh (1849–1905), when he wrote:

Muslims have neglected their religion and have become obsessed with the service of verbal forms. They have abandoned all the virtues and good qualities their religion contains, and have passed nothing on. God does not heed these prayers that they pray and does not accept a single one of their prostrations: they just go through the motions and mouth words without understanding what they mean and it does not occur to any of them that they are addressing God Almighty, glorifying him, acknowledging His divinity, and seeking guidance and succor from Him and Him alone. It is extraordinary that jurists from the four main schools of law, and maybe others too, have said that praying without presence of mind and submission to God counts as performance of the obligation to pray. What kind of talk is that? It is nonsense.

These words, however harsh they may be, affirm once again the for-gotten fact: the essence of Islam is the call for truth, justice, and freedom and everything else is less important. Passionate religiosity in Egypt is real and sincere but it rarely follows the right course. The main issue in Egypt is as clear as the sun: an appalling situation of corruption, oppression, and injustice that has lasted thirty years and has driven many Egyptians to sui-cide, crime, or emigration at any price. Now that the president has stayed in power for thirty years without a single real election, the stage is being set for his son to inherit power, as though great Egypt were just a poultry farm the father might bequeath to his sons. Isn't that the height of injus-tice? When we realize that injustice invalidates fasting and that winning back our usurped rights is more important than a thousand prostrations we make at special Ramadan prayers, only then will we have reached a true understanding of Islam. True Islam is democracy.

Democracy is the solution.

August 17, 2010

FREE SPEECH AND
STATE REPRESSION

How Do Police Officers
Celebrate Ramadan?

On August 23, 2007, at six o'clock in the morning, Mohamed Ali Hassan woke up to the sound of loud banging on the door of his home in Benhawi Street in Bab al-Sha'riya. His wife, Asma, and his two young children, Youssef and Mohamed, woke up terrified to the sight of security men hitting their father violently, then arresting him and taking him off to al-Daher police station. According to the testimony of Mohamed Ali Hassan's wife, the detectives at the police station arrested him and framed him on a drugs charge as a favor to two influential people in the neighborhood with whom Mohamed had had an argument a few days earlier.

Whether or not this story is true, the great month of Ramadan started with Mohamed Ali Hassan in custody at the police station. His wife Asma would visit him whenever the officers allowed. Then something unknown to us took place to arouse the wrath of the detectives against Mohamed the prisoner. The detectives ordered him to be beaten and tortured, and then incited some of the hardened criminals in the cell to attack him. They pounced on him and stabbed him with knives. After breaking the fast on the first Thursday of Ramadan, Mohamed's wife went to visit him at the police station and found him in very poor health. He was bleeding profusely and his face and body were covered with bruises and wounds. He could not speak or walk. Asma was horrified at the state of her husband and begged the police officers to let her take Mohamed under police escort to a hospital for treatment, even at the expense of the family. But the officers refused and threatened to detain her too if she did not leave immediately. The following day Mohamed Ali Hassan died from the injuries he received under torture.

In the same week, prisoner Hani al-Ghandour was detained in Assiut Prison pending trial in a criminal case. One of the officers working in the prison, a man by the name of Islam Bey, threw some insults at Hani and it seems that Hani answered back in a way that displeased Islam Bey, who decided to discipline him. Islam Bey summoned a detective called Ismail and the two of them put Hani in a hole in the earth and forced him to stay there for two hours while they gave him a violent beating. Then they tied Hani to a metal chair and started giving him electric shocks and beating him with bamboo sticks. In the end they brought a water hose and put it up his nose. When the torture reached its peak, Hani started screaming, "Enough, Islam Bey, I'm going to die . . . I can't take it." But Islam Bey, with his long experience of prisoners, was not about to fall for a trick like that. He went on giving Hani electric shocks and beating him until the prisoner finally breathed his last and died.

These two incidents were reported in the newspapers in the same week of Ramadan and, as usual, the Ministry of Interior issued a statement denying any torture had taken place and attributing the two deaths to the same cause: a sudden and sharp fall in blood pressure. Nobody believes such statements from the ministry and they are not even worth discussing, but these two incidents, apart from being so brutal, do raise some important questions. The officers who carried out the torture are Muslims (in fact one of them is called Islam) and are probably strict about fasting during Ramadan and performing their prayers on time. Maybe they perform the special prayers on Ramadan nights as well, like other people, but they also torture prisoners in this barbaric way without it troubling their religious conscience in the least. In fact it never occurs to them that torture is incompatible with fasting and prayer.

This is something really strange that deserves thought and study. How can a police officer torture people and then resume his life afterward as though nothing has happened? How can such an officer play with his children and sleep with his wife when his hands are still stained with the blood of his victims? How do talented and brilliant young men, physically fit and intellectually sharp, who enroll in the police academy and take an oath to respect the law, turn over time into brutes who enjoy torturing people and abusing them sexually? Does police work dispose officers toward some pathological sadism whereby they enjoy torturing other people?

Psychological studies show that many ordinary people, if they end up working in a place where torture takes place systematically, are very likely to get involved in torture and turn into torturers themselves. But first they have to go through two psychological processes: adaptation and moral justification. Adaptation means that the officer finds all his colleagues carrying out torture and his superiors ordering torture, so he obeys the orders and carries out torture because he is not strong enough to take a stand against the dominant practice where he works. Justification means that the officer who tortures people convinces himself that it is necessary for the sake of security and the nation. A torturer who fails to create a justification for himself will not be able to continue torturing people. Torture in Egypt is not the work of errant or rogue officers, it is a permanent and systematic policy applied by the state, and there have been more victims of torture in the Mubarak era than in any other period of Egyptian history.

When we were school children we all studied the Denshawai massacre, which took place in 1906, as evidence that the British occupation was a crime against Egyptians. We must remember unfortunately that the number of Egyptians killed in this famous massacre was only five (the English shot one woman dead and four men were hanged). Twice as many people or more die in police stations and on State Security premises in Egypt in one year or less, so what we Egyptians are doing to ourselves is much worse than what British soldiers did to us. Responsibility for the innocents who die of torture in Egypt does not lie solely with the officers who commit the crime of torture, or with Interior Minister Habib al-Adli, who gives them the orders. The prime responsibility lies with President Hosni Mubarak. He undoubtedly knows that people are tortured to death every day but he does not intervene or do anything to stop these crimes. If President Mubarak wanted to stop torture, it would stop within one hour, but he sees torture as necessary to protect the regime.

God have mercy on Hani al-Ghandour and Mohamed Ali Hassan from Bab al-Sha'riya. All condolences, in this holy month, to their families and their children, who are fated to grow up without fathers. But this injustice is too outrageous to continue. Someday soon all those responsible for these crimes and tragedies will be held to account, and the oppressors will find out what fate awaits them.

September 17, 2008

A Discussion with a State Security Officer

The following happened some years ago. I was at a relative's wedding and sat down next to a guest I had not met before. He introduced himself to me: "My name is . . . I am a police officer." He seemed to be in his forties, very elegant, polite, and quiet. I noticed a prayer mark on his forehead. After exchanging niceties, I asked him, "In which department do you work?" He hesitated for a second, then replied, "State Security." We were both silent and he turned his face away from me and started watching the guests. My mind was torn between two conflicting ideas: should I resume our small talk or express my opinion on State Security freely? In the end, I failed to exercise self-restraint and said, "Excuse me! You are religious, as I can see."

"Thank God."

"But don't you find any contradiction between being religious and working with State Security?"

"Where's the contradiction?"

"State Security detainees are beaten, tortured, and raped even though religions prohibit such practices."

He started to lose his temper. "First, those who are beaten deserve being beaten. Second, if you study your religion thoroughly, you will find that what we do at the State Security department is in harmony with Islamic teachings."

"But Islam strongly stresses the protection of human dignity."

"The case you are making is not correct. I am well acquainted with Islamic jurisprudence and its provisions."

"Islamic jurisprudence does not allow torturing people."

"Listen to me until I finish. Islam has nothing to do with democracy or elections. . . . Jurists made obeying the ruler a must whether he takes power via Muslims' consent or the use of force. The public should not challenge the ruler even if he is corrupt or unjust. Do you know how Islam punishes those who rebel against their rulers?"

I kept silent.

He replied enthusiastically, "They should face the *haraba* punishment, or cutting off the left hand and the right foot. All the detainees at State Security headquarters are insurgents whose feet and hands should be cut off in accordance with *sharia*. But we do not do this. We apply quite softer measures."

We had a long discussion. I argued that Islam takes the side of justice and freedom and that the Prophet Muhammad gave Muslims the freedom to choose his successor. Moreover, the meeting that led to Abu Bakr's succession was an ideally democratic experience that long preceded western democracy. I explained that *haraba* punishment should be confined to armed groups that kill and rape innocent people and plunder their property. It should by no means be applied to Egyptian political dissidents. He was persistent and ended the discussion by saying, "This is the way I understand Islam. I will not change it and I will be responsible for it before God."

After I left the wedding, I asked myself how such a smart and educated man could be driven by these misconceptions of Islam. Where did he get his wrong ideas? How could one think that God approves of torturing people and degrading them? I failed to find answers to these questions until, months later, I read a research paper entitled "The Psychology of Flagellants." The author argues that policemen who practice torture could be divided into two groups: some are psychopathic, meaning aggressive with no ethical values, and others, who are the majority, are psychologically balanced. When the latter leave the office, they become different people and treat others nicely and cordially. To be able to practice torture, however, two conditions are indispensable: submission and conviction. Submission implies that the police officer assures himself that he does not have a say in what he is doing for he must obey orders. As for conviction, the officer has to believe that torture is ethically and religiously legitimate. Hence the victims are viewed as agents of the enemy or infidels. Torture then becomes a righteous practice that protects the homeland and the public. The researcher concluded that, without conviction, the police officer cannot go on with torturing people, for at a certain point he will despise himself and suffer from insurmountable guilt.

I remembered my conversation with the State Security officer when I heard about the arrest of two members of the April 6 Movement: Omnia Taha and Sarah Mohamed Rezq. A Kafr al-Sheikh University security guard arrested the two young women and handed them over to State Security on the grounds that they incited their fellow students to strike. The prosecution accused them of plotting to overthrow the regime and ordered that they be remanded to custody for fifteen days.

The event poses a host of questions, including how a call for a strike by a young woman (less than twenty years old) could overthrow President Mubarak's regime. Moreover, calling for a strike is not a crime, as Egypt has signed many international conventions legitimizing strikes as one of the basic human rights. I felt really sad when I learned that the two students had been subjected to severe torture at the hands of a senior State Security officer. He beat them and tore off their clothes. I recalled the State Security officer at the wedding and asked myself: How could a man, who might have a wife and daughter, treat a woman, who might be as young as his daughter, with such brutality? How could he tolerate the guilt and look in the eyes of his wife and children? Didn't he feel shame that he beat such a helpless young woman? Could this be in accordance with the values of manhood, religion, or ethics? Does this practice maintain the prestige of the army and police?

The regime in Egypt is encountering an unprecedented wave of protest as life has become intolerable for large groups of the Egyptian public who are left without the most basic needs of a decent life. These groups now have no alternative but to take to the streets to defend their legitimate rights. As for the regime, which has proved incapable of introducing any kind of genuine reform, it pushes the police force into confrontation with the people, to suppress and torture them. Yet the regime ignores the reality that policemen are part of the Egyptian population whose great majority suffers from difficult living conditions.

When a regime becomes solely dependent on oppression, it fails to realize that the apparatus of oppression, however mighty it may be, consists of individuals who are part of society and who share the grievances and interests of the rest of the population. As oppression deepens, these individuals will find they are unable to justify their crimes to themselves. Then the regime's iron grip will be broken and meet the fate it deserves. Where Egypt is concerned, I believe that day will come soon.

April 7, 2009

Four Videos to Entertain
President Mubarak

The two great leaders, President Hosni Mubarak and President Barack Obama, met recently in Washington, D.C. for friendly and fruitful talks in which they dealt with critical matters of interest to their two countries: Iran's nuclear program, peace with Israel, and the situation in Darfur. With equal vehemence the two presidents said how upset they were about the deterioration of the human rights situation in Iran, the repression of demonstrators, election rigging, the torture of innocent people, and other horrendous crimes perpetrated by the Iranian government, all of which the international community and the Egyptian government are making intensive efforts to expose and prevent. In the end President Obama received assurances from his friend, President Mubarak, that while democratic reform in Egypt is a long and complicated process it is continuing and hopefully will never come to a halt. Obama reiterated his admiration for President Mubarak's wisdom, moderation, and courage.

All of that is well-known, understandable, and to be expected, but I was thinking of something else. The journey from Washington to Cairo takes more than ten hours, so how does President Mubarak spend that time? The president's private plane is no doubt equipped to the highest possible standard, but it's nonetheless a long journey, so what does the president do on the way? Does he take the opportunity to snatch a few hours' sleep so that his body can recover from all the exhausting work he does? Does he spend the time in conversation with the government newspaper editors whom he takes along with him on every trip? As usual, they would compete to praise the president's achievements, his historic leadership, and the excellence of his decisions. I think that the president must be somewhat bored by repeated praise. Does he enjoy some reading during the journey? Does he take along the collected works of Mahmoud Sami al-Baroudi, whom he has cited as his favorite poet? I don't know exactly what the president likes to do, so I suggest he watch some good videos, which I hope he likes. Not long feature films, but short documentaries in which the performers are not professional actors or even amateurs but just ordinary Egyptians with nothing to distinguish them except that, like millions of other Egyptians, they face a bitter daily struggle to feed their children and provide them with a decent life. Here are the videos I suggest.

In the first video we see a young Egyptian from Port Said being horribly tortured in a police station. The young man appears in the first shot with the skin on his back and stomach flayed from a beating, lifted up and hung from the ceiling by his hands. The man starts to beg the police officers for mercy, saying, "Enough, Mohamed Bey! I'm going to die, Mohamed Bey." In the second shot the young man appears blindfolded, weeping and imploring the officer in a broken voice, "I beg you, Mohamed Bey. We're human beings, not animals." We can't see Mohamed Bey in the shot but we can hear his angry voice as he shouts, "Shut up!" at the man and then hurls the most vicious insults at him. Why does Mohamed Bey seem so angry? The reason is that the young man has been screaming under torture and Mohamed Bey sees this as an affront to his status because, according to the rules as he sees them, no one has the right to speak up in front of a police officer even if the officer is beating and torturing him.

The second video has a woman as the main character: an Egyptian woman in her thirties, her hair uncovered, wearing blue jeans and a dark t-shirt. The police officer appears with a big stick, beating her mercilessly. He is beating her all over with all his strength, on her feet, her arms, and her head. The woman screams and then falls silent and then in the next shot we see her strung up horizontally with her hands and feet tied to a metal pole. This is the position people say is used in police stations and on State Security premises and is known as the 'chicken position.' It causes horrific pain, tears the muscles, and can lead to bone and even spinal fractures. Not content with stringing her up in the 'chicken position,' the policeman carries on hitting her with his big stick until she cries out at the top of her voice, "Okay, pasha, it was me who killed him, it was me who killed him." At this point we realize that the policeman is investigating a murder and that by this very effective method he has identified the murderer and justice has been done.

In the third video we see a man in his forties trembling in fear in front of a police officer, who is hurling the most vile insults at him. The policeman then raises his hand and brings it down forcefully toward the man's face. Just as the man shuts his eyes against the blow, the policeman freezes his hand in the air then wiggles his fingers obscenely. The policeman breaks into sustained laughter and walks around the room triumphantly as though he has just pulled off some clever trick. Then the policeman gets serious again, approaches the man with a cigarette in the corner of his mouth, and starts slapping his face repeatedly with both hands. When the man raises a hand instinctively to fend off the blows, the policeman stops, insults the man's mother, and tells him to put his hand back down at his side. Then he starts slapping him again.

In the fourth film we don't see the policeman because he's sitting behind the camera. Instead we see a man more than sixty years old, frail and obviously poor and malnourished. A muscular police informer has grabbed him and we hear the officer saying to the informer, "Hit him, Abdel Rasoul." Abdel Rasoul carries out the order and starts to lay into the old man. But the policeman, whose voice sounds serene and playful, says, "That's very gentle, Abdel Rasoul, too gentle. Hit him hard." Abdel Rasoul hits the man more and more violently as the policeman tells him where to strike. "Give it to him on the back of the neck, Abdel Rasoul. Now hit him on the head." Abdel Rasoul tries hard to please the officer and hits harder and harder, but the officer tut-tuts and says, "Your performance is very feeble, Abdel Rasoul." At that point another informer comes into the room to help Abdel Rasoul do his job, and the two of them beat up the old man, trying to prove their competence to the officer. The old man submits to their blows to the extent that he cannot raise his hand or even scream. He looks vacant, as though he is dead.

Mr. President, I chose these films from the many available on Wael Abbas' blog, "Egyptian Awareness," and many other blogs on the Internet. All of them are authentic visual and audio records of the terrifying crimes of torture to which Egyptians are subjected daily. In many cases the names of the officers and the places where they work are available along with the video. In most cases the faces of the officers are clearly visible in the image, which would make it easy to identify them. All of these videos were recorded on cell phones by people who happened to be present during the torture sessions, and were somehow leaked to the blogs. Sometimes the police officer videoed himself as he was doing the torturing, to show the images to his colleagues or to humiliate the victims or intimidate them in the future. Humans are normally inclined to record the happy moments in their lives. It makes sense that one would photograph one's wedding or graduation ceremony, but to record oneself as one tortures people is bizarre behavior, the motives for which psychiatrists might help us understand.

Mr. President, I am not asking you to intervene to stop this degradation to which dozens of Egyptians are subjected daily in police stations and on State Security premises. I am not asking you to investigate the crimes of torture committed against innocents by people who represent the regime you head. I am not asking you to intervene because, like all Egyptians, I have learned from experience the limits of what is possible in Egypt. I only wanted to recommend some films to entertain Your Excellency on your long journey. Mr. President, have a safe trip.

Democracy is the solution.

August 18, 2009

Before We Damn Switzerland

On October 27 I was on a visit to Switzerland and wrote about the battle over minarets for the first time. I said that the gravity of this battle went beyond banning minarets because it would lead to the passage of a law in which Islam is officially linked with terrorism and because it would open the door to more legal campaigns by right-wing racist parties aimed at restricting the freedoms of Muslims in the West. In my article I advocated forming a delegation of professors of Islamic civilization and enlightened men of religion to travel to Switzerland in order to explain to the public that the minaret is an Islamic architectural feature and not an emblem of war, as alleged by the right-wing Swiss People's Party, which started this battle. *Al-Shorouk* newspaper responded to my suggestion and contacted senior officials in Egypt, but it appears they were not enthusiastic about the idea or were enthusiastic but did not do anything about it, except for the mufti of the republic, whose media adviser happened to be invited to a conference in Switzerland and came back after the vote on banning minarets was over. The truth is that the failure of Egyptian officials to do their duty has become a frequent and saddening phenomenon. In the events surrounding the football match between Egypt and Algeria in Sudan, we saw how the Egyptian authorities were unable to protect Egyptian citizens from the barbaric assault committed by Algerian criminal gangs sent over on military planes by the Algerian government, and how after that they were unable to hold to account those who affronted the dignity of Egyptians.

A few days ago, the referendum result went against us and minarets were banned by law in Switzerland. Egyptians felt angered and wondered how Switzerland could claim to be a democratic country and at the same time prevent Muslims, not members of other religious communities, from building minarets. They asked what harm there is in minarets and why the Swiss do not want to see them in their country. Could similar measures be taken against, for example, Jewish synagogues in Switzerland? The anger of Egyptians is natural and understandable and their questions are legitimate, but before we damn Switzerland we should remember several facts:

First, the ban on minarets in Switzerland does not at all mean that the Swiss have all taken a position against Islam. Almost half the Swiss voters, as well as Swiss government officials and representatives of Christian and Jewish communities of all sects, vigorously defended until the last moment the right of Muslims to build their minarets. In fact, the referendum result led to demonstrations in many Swiss cities in defense of the right of Muslims to practice their religious rites. I received many letters from cultured Swiss friends expressing their deep regret at the ban on minarets, including one from the prominent critic, Angela Schader, who wrote, "I am shocked and ashamed for my country," and described the ban as "a decision that is stupid, narrow-minded, and cowardly."

Second, although the referendum is legal and binding under the Swiss constitution, it violates the principles of human rights and a case can be pursued in international forums with a view to overturning the ban. This is the right way to deal with the problem. Calling for boycotts and accusing Switzerland of hostility to Islam would indicate an unfair perception of the Swiss people and would lead to mutual hostility from which only the extremists there would benefit.

Third, the Swiss People's Party, which provoked this crisis, is one of many right-wing European parties, all of which have racist messages hostile to foreigners and immigrants. The People's Party has exploited Swiss people's fear of Islam and their ignorance of its tolerant teachings, and with this referendum it has taken a step that will be followed by other steps. Party officials have stated that they are preparing new referendums against wearing the *hijab* at work and in educational institutions, against female circumcision, and against separate cemeteries for Muslims. French President Nicolas Sarkozy was quick to support the ban on minarets and said he understood the need for western society to preserve its cultural identity, and voices soon arose in the Netherlands and Germany calling for similar referendums to restrain Muslims. So the battle has not ended with the ban on minarets. It has only started, and we must defend the rights of Muslims by means that are legal, effective, and respectful.

Fourth, from my long experience of western society I believe that we as Muslims are responsible to a large extent for the powerful wave of fear of Islam. This feeling did not exist, or at least was not evident, before the attacks of 9/11. Criminal terrorists such as Osama bin Laden and Ayman al-Zawahiri took it upon themselves to tarnish the image of Islam in the minds of millions of westerners. Suffice it to say that the word 'jihad' is now used in western languages to mean armed attacks on civilians and that the term 'islamisme' in French has come to mean terrorism, even in academic circles. Add to this the fact that most mosques in the West are financed by Wahhabi oil sheikhs who offer an extreme Salafist interpretation of the religion, which has very much helped to distort its image in western minds. It is enough to know that physical education classes for Muslim girls have become a big problem in Swiss schools because many Muslim parents insist on preventing their young daughters from taking part in physical education and swimming classes (based on erroneous Wahhabi *fatwa*s of course). This forces the school authorities to defend the right of girls to take part and at the same time reinforces the image of Islam as a reactionary religion that sees women only as bodies that cause temptation and are to be used for pleasure. One has to imagine the reaction of westerners when they hear that Islam requires female circumcision (a horrendous crime that has nothing to do with Islam) or when they see a woman wearing the *niqab*, or face veil, whether with two eye openings or only one, as some Saudi sheikhs advocate. Wahhabi ideas, backed by oil money, provide the worst possible image of Islam to western minds. Those who voted in favor of the ban on minarets in Switzerland are not all racists; they are simply afraid of a religion linked in their minds with violence, murder, backwardness, and the oppression of women. It is our duty to offer the West the correct image of Islam, which created a great civilization that for seven centuries taught the whole world the principles of justice, freedom, and tolerance. If we fail in performing this duty then we will have no right to blame others.

Fifth, the banning of minarets in Switzerland is clearly a flagrant violation of freedom of belief, and Egyptians, Arabs, and Muslims have a right to object to the ban and to try to overturn it by all legal means. But the Egyptian government has no moral right to object to the ban on minarets in Switzerland because it has failed to ensure freedom of belief for Egyptians. The Egyptian authorities regularly arrest Shi'ites and Qur'anists, put them on trial on charges of contempt for religion, and throw them in prison. In fact, the official department headed by the mufti, which is now calling for freedom of belief in Switzerland, has issued an official *fatwa* declaring Baha'is to be infidels, putting them in danger of being murdered at any moment. These Baha'is are Egyptian citizens who have fought a bitter battle for recognition of their religion in official documents. As for the Coptic Christians, they face the greatest hardship when they try to build new churches or even repair old ones. A uniform law for places of worship that would put mosques and churches on the same legal basis has been buried for many years in the files of the Egyptian government, which refuses even to discuss it.

Freedom of belief means guaranteeing respect and freedom of worship for everyone, whatever their beliefs and their religion. This is just the opposite of what the Egyptian government does. It cannot demand freedom of belief in Switzerland while obstructing it in Egypt. The Egyptian regime, which holds power through repression and fraud, cannot guarantee freedom of belief for its citizens because if you have lost something you cannot then give it away and because freedom of belief will not come about in isolation from other public freedoms and political rights.

Democracy is the solution.

December 6, 2009

An Unfortunate Incident Befalls
a State Security Officer

Last Saturday Amr Bey, an officer in State Security, finished his work unusually early and hurried home. He was happy because he would see his only daughter, Nourhan, who is ten years old and whom he rarely sees during the week. He usually comes home from work after she has gone to bed and when he wakes up she's already at school. Amr Bey came in and greeted his wife, Nadia, who was in the kitchen, and then quickly headed to his daughter's room. He opened the door and found her studying. She was wearing a blue work-out outfit and had her hair in a ponytail. He kissed her on the forehead and asked if she had had dinner. She said she would have dinner when she finished her homework. Amr Bey told her he would eat with her, then put out his right hand and patted her on the cheek. Suddenly Nourhan looked terrified and shouted, "Papa, there's blood on your hand!" Amr Bey looked at his right hand and to his amazement found it covered with congealed blood. Nourhan screamed in horror and her mother rushed in from the kitchen to find out what was happening. Amr Bey kept his cool and tried to reassure his wife and daughter. He went into the bathroom quickly and washed his hand with hot water and soap several times until he had removed all traces of blood. Then he dried it with a towel.

When he came out of the bathroom he found Nadia waiting for him. He kissed her on the cheek and smiled to reassure her. The couple went into the bedroom and Amr Bey started to take off his suit to put on his pajamas and go to bed. But as soon as he looked at his hand he shouted, "Nadia, the blood's come back!" It was no longer possible to ignore what

173

was happening. Nadia dressed hurriedly and took him off in her car. Amr sat next to her and tried to contact the director of Salam Hospital, whom he knew well. He was holding his cell phone in his left hand because his right hand was completely covered in congealed blood. On the way to the hospital Amr began to wonder where all this blood on the palm of his right hand was coming from. He hadn't injured himself and he didn't remember bumping his hand into anything.

Amr Bey mentally went over everything he had done that day. He had arrived at the State Security offices at 1 p.m. and before going to his office he had dropped in on his colleague, Tamer Bey, to make sure he had booked his summer vacation in Marsa Matrouh for August 1, so they could spend it together. Tamer Bey was in the same year as Amr at college and was one of his closest friends. Amr Bey went into Tamer's office and found him busy interrogating some Islamists who were members of the Wa'd (Promise) group. He saw a man hanging upside down by his feet—the position known as the *dabiha*, or sacrificial victim—as the detectives gave him repeated electric shocks between his legs. The man was screaming in a horrifying way, while Tamer's voice boomed through the room. "You know what, momma's boy, if you don't confess, I'll bring your wife, Bothaina, strip her naked, and have the soldiers do her in front of your eyes," he said. As soon as Tamer Bey caught sight of his friend, Amr Bey, his face lit up and he rushed to shake his hand. Then Tamer took him aside and assured him he had made the booking.

Amr Bey came out of Tamer Bey's office and decided to say good morning to his colleague, Abdel Khalek Bey, who was interrogating cement plant workers who were on strike. Amr Bey went in and saw a man dressed only in his underwear, tied by the hands and feet, as though crucified, to a piece of wood they call "the Doll." The man's body was covered with bruises and wounds. Behind him stood a detective thrashing him with a whip while other detectives were busy beating him violently about the head and face. Abdel Khalek started shouting at him, "So you're acting the militant and the hero, are you? Very well, momma's boy, I swear I'm going to make you kiss the soldiers' boots. I'll make you wish you were dead, but you won't be able to die." Amr Bey greeted his friend, Abdel Khalek, from afar and hurried off so as not to distract him from his work.

After that Amr Bey settled down in his office, where he interrogated two young men from the April 6 Movement who had been inviting people in the street to come out and welcome Dr. Mohamed ElBaradei at the airport. The interrogation was easy because the men had arrived in his office completely exhausted after detectives beat and whipped them through the night, and in fact Amr Bey didn't have much to do. He gave the men the usual barrage of insults and was about to dismiss them, but he noticed that one of them was looking at him with a certain defiance. He stood up from behind his desk and slapped him on the face several times. This was the signal for the detectives to start a new barrage of kicks and cuffs. At this point Amr Bey shouted at the man, "Say, 'I'm a woman.' Come on!" The brutal beating continued but the young man refused to say, "I'm a woman." Amr Bey gave an order and the detectives started to drag the man about by his feet, with his head banging against the floor as they hit him with their fists and heavy boots until he lost consciousness.

That's all Amr Bey had done during the day. He went over it in his mind and did not see anything strange or unfamiliar in it. Quite an ordinary day. So where did this congealed blood come from? Amr Bey arrived at the hospital and found the director waiting for him in person. He gave him a thorough check-up and took a blood sample, which was analyzed immediately. With Amr Bey and his wife, Nadia, sitting in his office, the director read the results of the analysis several times, then took off his glasses and said, "Look, sir. People bleed from the palm of the hand in three cases: because of a wound, or because of an overdose of anticoagulants, or, God forbid, because they have a malignant blood disease. You're not injured, you haven't taken any anticoagulants, and the blood looks healthy. The fact is, sir, that your case is odd. Let's wait twenty-four hours and hopefully the bleeding will stop."

The hospital director prescribed some drugs, gave the officer some bandages to stop his hand from bleeding, and asked him to stop by in the morning for a check-up. Amr Bey did not sleep all night and in the morning he heard his daughter, Nourhan, as she prepared for school. He decided not to go out and see her in case she was frightened by the sight of his bloody hand. He dressed with the help of his wife, who again went with him to the hospital director, who examined him and repeated with regret that there was no medical explanation for the bleeding. The director asked Amr Bey to continue with the drugs and the bandages.

Amr Bey went back home, called the office, and told them he was ill and would not come in that day. He spent a full day in his room, eating nothing despite his wife's insistence. He would sleep only for a few minutes before waking up to look at his hand and finding it always stained with blood. The next morning his wife came in and found him stretched out on the bed, apparently completely exhausted. But on his face she also saw a new and strange expression. Amr Bey struggled to his feet, dressed with his wife's help, and asked her to drive him to the office. There he went to the office of the general who was the director of State Security investigations and asked to see him. They let him in straight away. The general welcomed him and was upset when he saw the bandages on his right hand. "Hope it's not serious, Amr. What's the problem?"

Amr Bey told the general what had happened and the general scowled. "Strange story," he said. "Anyway, take time off until you're better." But Amr Bey smiled and with his left hand produced a piece of paper that he placed on the desk in front of the general. The general read it quickly and then cried out in disapproval, "What's all this? Have you gone mad, Amr? Would anyone leave State Security?"

"I implore you, sir."

"Give yourself a chance to think, my son. You're one of the best officers in the department and you have a great future. Can you tell me why you want to leave the department?"

At that point, without speaking, Amr Bey held his bloody right hand in front of the general's face.

Democracy is the solution.

March 7, 2010

Why Was the General Screaming?

The young men and women who came out to demonstrate in the streets of Cairo on April 6 did not break the law or do anything wrong. They only wanted to express their opinion. They were demanding freedom, justice, dignity, fair elections, the abolition of the emergency law, and constitutional amendments to ensure equal opportunities for all Egyptians to stand in elections. All of these demands are just and legitimate. So why were these youngsters abused and beaten, dragged off and detained? No respectable state in the world punishes its citizens in this brutal way just for expressing their opinions. What happened on April 6 will remain a shameful stain on the reputation of the Egyptian regime forever. The youngsters were surrounded by a cordon of riot police, who pressed in on them until they almost suffocated them, then the karate units of the police pounced on them, hitting the demonstrators on the head and body with thick sticks. I have never seen such barbaric methods used on protesters, other than by the Israeli army against Palestinian demonstrators during the Intifada. Why do Egyptians attack fellow Egyptians with such brutality? The young people were screaming and some had such serious injuries that the asphalt was covered with their blood, but the beatings did not stop.

Finally a man in his fifties appeared, well-built, swarthy, and dressed in civilian clothes, with a large prayer mark on his forehead. The man, addressed as "General" by the policemen, gave orders that the girls be taken out of the cordoned area one by one. "Bring me that whore over there," he shouted to his assistants in a voice like thunder. Immediately the men rushed off to drag the girl away from her colleagues. The youngsters fought hard to defend the girl, protecting her with their bodies and shielding her from assault, but the police attacked with such ferocity and inflicted so many injuries that in the end their resistance flagged and the police managed to remove the girl. They pushed her from behind and hit her until she was standing facing the general, who greeted her with a barrage of vulgar insults. He raised his hand and slapped her several times, then grabbed her *hijab* and removed it. Then he took hold of her hair and dragged her along the ground, kicking her as hard as he could as he went until he threw her toward a group of policemen, who kept hitting, slapping, and kicking her until finally they dumped her, a total wreck, in the police wagon. The image of the general attacking girls in the same way appears in all the video material that escaped confiscation by the police.

But I noticed something strange: while the general was attacking the girl and dragging her off, his face was contorted and he was incessantly screaming. He was making strange rasping, guttural noises as though it were he who was in pain, and I wondered: Why is the general screaming? It's obvious why the girl would scream when she was being savaged in the streets within view of all the passersby. But the general who was hitting her, why would he scream? He was strong, powerful, and in complete control of the situation. He had everything in his favor while the poor girl had nothing. His word was law and he could do what he wanted with the girl: hit her, slap her, drag her along the ground. Even if he killed her no one would punish him. So why was he screaming? In war a fighter might scream out loud in battle to frighten the enemy, but the general was not at war and he was not facing an armed enemy. He was attacking a defenseless girl who was almost dying of fright, pain, and a sense of humiliation and shame. Was the general screaming as he attacked the girl in order to overcome the reservations of his subordinate police officers, some of whom might refuse to assault an innocent Egyptian girl who had not committed a crime or broken the law? Was he screaming in order to forget that his real duty was to protect this girl from assault rather than to assault her himself?

Was he screaming in order to forget that this girl, whose *hijab* he had removed and whom he was dragged along the ground, was just like his own daughter, whom he no doubt loves and cherishes and whom he would never allow to be insulted or harmed? If his own daughter had a difficult exam or just had a simple cold, the general would not be able to sleep without checking on her. Was he screaming because when he graduated from the police academy thirty years ago, he had dreams of upholding the law and justice and swore to protect the dignity, lives, and property of

Egyptians, and then little by little he had been drawn into protecting the Mubarak regime, until in the end his mission was to abuse girls?

Perhaps he was screaming because he is religious, or at least considers himself religious, because he prays and fasts regularly, even performs the dawn prayer on time whenever he can, has gone on the *hajj* and on the lesser pilgrimage more than once, and has had the prayer mark on his forehead for years from all his prostrations. Perhaps he was screaming because he knows that he is over fifty and his death may come at any moment. He might die in a traffic accident or he might be struck down by some serious disease, or even, as happens with many people, he might go to bed one night in the best of health and in the morning his wife tries to wake him up and finds him dead. The general knows for sure that he will die and will stand before God, who will hold him to account, and on that day neither President Mubarak nor Interior Minister Habib al-Adli will be able to do him any good, nor even the prosecutor general, who has been shelving all the complaints against him for lack of sufficient evidence. On the great Day of Judgment, everyone will abandon him—the bodyguards, the informers, the riot police, the officers, his friends, his wife, and even his children. On that day his general's rank will do him no good, nor his ties to senior officials, nor his wealth. On that day he will stand as naked as the day his mother gave birth to him, weak and defenseless. He will tremble in fear at the judgment of the Creator.

On that day God will ask him, "Why did you assault a poor Egyptian girl who could not defend herself? Why did you hit her, drag her along the ground, and abuse her in public? Would you like it if someone did that to your daughter?" What will the general say then? He cannot tell God he was carrying out orders. Orders will not absolve him or spare him God's punishment for the crimes he has committed, despite the general's authority and influence, despite the tens of thousands of riot police and thugs and police karate units that, like vicious trained dogs, await one signal from him before they beat and abuse innocent people. In spite of all this overwhelming power, the general felt deep inside as he assaulted the girl that he was weak and wretched and unable to control himself and that little by little he was being drawn into committing horrendous crimes in order to protect President Hosni Mubarak and his family.

The general felt that the girl he was beating was stronger than him because she was defending truth and justice, because she was innocent, noble, pure, and brave, and because she loved her country and would defend it with all her strength. As they dragged her along the ground, kicking her with their boots, she did not beg, or call for help, or appeal to the brutes. She was chanting: "Freedom, freedom, long live Egypt, long live Egypt." And at that point the general had a strange feeling. He realized that he could kill this girl, tear her body apart if he wanted, but he could never defeat her, or humiliate her, or break her will. He felt that despite all his power he was defeated and that it was this poor abused and violated girl who would triumph. At that point all the general could do was scream.

Democracy is the solution.

April 12, 2010

Should We Start with Moral Reform
or Reforming the System?

Two illustrative incidents from my student days come to mind in discussing professional standards, morality, and corruption. The first incident occurred when I was studying dentistry at Cairo University. At the end of the year we had to take theoretical and practical exams, followed by an oral examination that was the magical gateway to favoritism and the misuse of influence. I remember that a fellow student in my year, a woman by the name of Hala, had a father who was a professor of medicine at a provincial university and so was friends with most of the professors responsible for the exams. As luck would have it, I went to the oral examination on physiology together with Hala and another woman student. The professor asked me a barrage of difficult questions, which I managed to answer. He then grilled the other woman with abstruse questions, and she stumbled and could not answer. When it was Hala's turn the professor looked at her, sitting next to me, and said sympathetically, "How are you, Hala? Send my regards to your father." He then told her she could leave. I came out of the appointment feeling humiliated and wronged, because I had passed a difficult exam while the professor had not asked Hala any questions at all. When the results came out, Hala and I were graded 'excellent' in physiology; in my case because I gave good answers during the exam and in Hala's case because she sent the professor's regards to her father.

The other incident took place some years later at the University of Illinois while I was studying for a master's degree. The statistics professor was a white racist woman who hated Arabs and Muslims, and although I completed the final exam with no mistakes I was surprised to find that she gave me a 'very good' grade, instead of the 'excellent' I deserved. I complained to one of my American colleagues and she advised me to read the university regulations and to make an appointment to see the professor. I read the regulations and discovered that students who felt unfairly treated in exams had the right to submit a complaint against the professor, in which case the university would appoint an external group of professors to review the exam paper. If the student's complaint was unjustified the university would not take any measures against him (the aim of that provision was to make sure that students were not too intimidated to complain), and if the student's complaint was justified the result would be changed at once and a formal warning would be sent to the professor responsible. If a professor received three such warnings, his or her contract would be automatically invalidated. I went to see the bigoted professor and after discussing it with her I was certain she had treated me unfairly. Calmly, I told her that in accordance with the university regulations I wanted to photocopy the answer paper because I was going to submit a complaint against her. This sentence had a magical effect: she paused for some moments and then said she needed to review the paper carefully. When I went back to her at the end of the day, as she had requested, the secretary told me she had adjusted my grade to 'excellent.'

After that I thought long about the significance of these two incidents. The bigoted American professor was just as unfair as the Egyptian professor, but she failed to have her way because the regulations at the University of Illinois protect the rights of students and punish anyone who treats them unfairly, regardless of rank. The regulations at Cairo University, on the other hand, give professors full authority over students, so they can do what they like with impunity. The factor that brings about justice in any society is the application of the law against powerful people rather than against the small. What happened to me at Cairo University is what happens right across Egypt. Many people obtain things they do not deserve as a result of their personal connections or their ability to pay bribes, or because the security agencies or the ruling party have selected them. But most Egyptians live in inhumane conditions—poverty, disease, complete despair about the future—and the law in Egypt is usually applied only against the weak, who cannot escape it or obstruct it. The junior civil servant caught taking a few hundred Egyptian pounds in bribes is tried and thrown in jail, whereas nobody touches the senior civil servant who takes commissions worth millions. Given this widespread injustice, it is pointless to urge people to act ethically without changing the corrupt system that pushes them to be dishonest.

Some years ago a well-known television program on a government channel invited me to talk about the phenomenon of bribes in Egypt, and I was surprised when the presenter portrayed bribery as merely a moral failing caused only by a flawed conscience and weak faith. I told the presenter that what he said is true but that it is not enough to explain bribery, which cannot be studied without discussing the level of wages and prices. He strongly objected and ended the interview early. In fact what that presenter did is the same as what all government officials do: portray ethics as invariable, completely divorced from social and political circumstances. Generally they attribute Egypt's current tribulations to the poor morals of Egyptians themselves. Perhaps we can now understand why President Mubarak is always accusing Egyptians of being lazy and unproductive. Such thinking ignores the fact that productivity in any country requires a good education, equal job opportunities, and salaries that allow a decent standard of living. All these tasks President Mubarak's regime has completely failed to accomplish for Egyptians.

In the same context we can now understand the recent behavior of Minister of Education Ahmed Zaki Badr, who is already infamous as the president of Ain Shams University who brought armed thugs to beat up students protesting on campus. Badr, accompanied by journalists and television cameras, has been making surprise visits to schools, where he abuses teachers who are absent or turn up late. He appears on camera lecturing teachers on the virtues of discipline, as if God created some good teachers who are disciplined and other teachers who are evil and lax by nature and who need to be severely punished until they learn to be disciplined. This perverse logic ignores the fact that government schools have no supplies, no equipment, and no laboratories, and the teachers receive such derisory salaries that they have to beg from those who pay them for private lessons or look for a second job so that they can provide for their own children. The minister does not want to see or hear all this because it would imply that he has a duty to carry out real reform, which he is unable to do. So he just lectures us on morals in isolation from any other considerations.

The same logic has been adopted by minister of Health Hatem al-Gabali, who is one of the giants of private sector investment in medicine in Egypt, as well as the man most responsible for public hospitals deteriorating to the point that instead of treating and caring for the poor their function is to finish them off and send them to the next world. Amid this decline, the minister, always accompanied by journalists and cameras, makes surprise visits to public hospitals and appears on the front pages of newspapers berating doctors who come in late and lecturing them on a doctor's humanitarian vocation. Of course he overlooks the fact that under his fine supervision these hospitals lack the most basic medical facilities, that rats and various insects are making merry throughout them, and that these wretched doctors are not paid enough to provide for their children and have to work day and night in private clinics to earn in a full month what His Excellency the minister earns from his private hospitals in minutes.

Appealing for moral reform in isolation from political reform, besides being naïve and unproductive, prevents a clear understanding of the situation and distracts people from the real reasons for decline. We cannot ask people to do their duty when they do not enjoy the most basic rights. We cannot hold people accountable until we provide them with a minimum of justice. I am not trying to justify corruption and I know there is always a category of outstanding people who are immune to corruption, however bad things get. But the morality of most people is influenced by the system that governs them. When someone senses justice it brings out the best human traits in him, and by the same token if he feels wronged or desperate then he is liable to be immoral and aggressive toward others. However eloquent our sermons may be, we will not wipe out prostitution until we wipe out poverty and we will never get rid of bribery and corruption until we set up a fair system that gives everyone his due and punishes wrongdoers, however powerful and influential they may be. Political reform is the first step forward and everything else is a waste of time and effort.

Democracy is the solution.

April 26, 2010

Are Freedoms Inseparable?

This is an important issue. A group of lawyers in Egypt recently filed a lawsuit in favor of confiscating the book, *A Thousand and One Nights*, on the grounds that it contains obscenities. Obviously these lawyers have never read the classics, as most classical works contain graphic details of relations between men and women, including *Kitab al-aghani* (The Book of Songs) by Abu al-Faraj al-Isfahani, *Kitab al-imta' wa-l-mu'anasa* (The Book of Enjoyment and Conviviality) by Abu Hayyan al-Tawhidi, and others. Even al-Jahiz (781–869 CE), the undisputed master of Arabic prose, wrote a famous epistle entitled "Mufakhara bayna ashab al-ghilman wa ashab al-jawari" (Debate between Owners of Concubines and Owners of Ephebes), in which a man who likes young boys has a discussion with a man who likes women. The work contains some obscenities but remains a beautiful and exquisite literary text. Censoring the great Arabic literary heritage opens the gates of hell to destroying and mutilating it. We must preserve our great heritage as it is. Even if we print expurgated texts that can be taught to adolescents and youngsters, the original texts must be maintained without any changes or deletions. That is my opinion and that is why I enthusiastically joined those defending freedom of literary expression against censorship and reactionary ideas.

But a difference of opinion did arise later, because in the middle of intellectuals' battle to defend *A Thousand and One Nights* the Egyptian government announced that it was extending the emergency law, which means that the natural law that protects the freedom and dignity of Egyptians will be suspended. I expected the champions of freedom defending *A Thousand and One Nights* to go out of their way to defend freedom in general, but unfortunately this did not happen. Many of the intellectuals defending *A Thousand and One Nights* today never open their mouths in protest at rigged elections or detentions or torture, all of which are horrendous crimes perpetrated by the Mubarak regime against millions of Egyptians. So I find myself wondering: Are freedoms inseparable? Can one defend the freedom of creativity in isolation from general freedom? Can intellectuals limit their role to matters related to writing while saying nothing about the country and people in general?

It's unfortunate that we even need to ask this question. In the world as a whole and in Egypt in the past, intellectuals always took a coherent position in overall defense of truth, justice, and freedom. The examples are countless: Abbas al-Akkad, Taha Hussein, Alfred Farag, and Abdel Rahman al-Sharqawi among Arab writers, and in the West Albert Camus, Jean-Paul Sartre, Bertrand Russell, Gabriel García Márquez, José Saramago, Pablo Neruda, and many other great creative artists who stood firmly against injustice and despotism and often paid a heavy price for the positions they took. In fact the most important novelist in the history of literature, the great Russian Fyodor Dostoyevsky (1821–1881), took part in public life and joined a secret organization to end Tsarist rule in Russia, for which he was arrested and sentenced to death, though the sentence was commuted at the last moment to four years in prison in Siberia. The essence of literary creation is the defense of noble human values, so how can a writer defend freedom in his books and then stay silent about violations of freedom in his daily life? The intellectual must lose all credibility if he puts his talents at the service of tyrants and never objects to injustice, corruption, the theft of public funds, and the oppression of the innocent, but at the same time waxes indignant in defense of a poem that is banned or a book that is confiscated.

Evidence for this is what recently happened in Libya when officials realized that the Gaddafi regime had a terrible reputation, as tens of thousands of innocent Libyans have been detained, tortured, expelled, or murdered simply because they have ideas contrary to the policies of Colonel Gaddafi (who recently decided to grant himself the title King of Kings of Africa). Libyan officials wanted to do something to polish the regime's image in the eyes of the world, and because Libya is a rich oil-producing country and because the money of the Libyan people is under the control of Colonel Gaddafi to spend as he likes without any oversight, they created a big literary prize called the Gaddafi Prize for International Literature with a value of 150,000 euros, to be awarded each year to a major international writer in order to improve the regime's image. In the first year they chose the great Spanish novelist, Juan Goytisolo, aged seventy-nine, whom critics consider to be the most important living Spanish writer. Goytisolo himself has suffered oppression, as the dictatorial Franco regime killed his mother when he was a child and forced him to live most of his life in exile. Goytisolo is also one of the greatest defenders of democracy and freedom, a big supporter of Arab rights, and such an admirer of Arab culture that he has lived permanently in Marrakesh for years. The Libyan officials contacted Goytisolo, congratulated him, and told him he had won the Gaddafi Prize for International Literature. In response Goytisolo wrote a letter to the adjudication committee, published in the Spanish newspaper *El País*, in which he turned down the prize and said:

> I have spent my life defending the right of Arab peoples to justice and freedom and I have stood firmly against the despotic regimes which through their corruption and injustice have kept millions of Arabs in the clutches of ignorance and poverty. . . . I can never accept a prize awarded by Colonel Gaddafi, who took power by force and established a dictatorial regime which detained, tortured and murdered innocent Libyans. I turn down this prize simply because it goes against all the principles I believe in.

This response was a slap in the face of the Gaddafi regime that echoed around the world. The London newspaper, *The Independent*, published a long article by Boyd Tonkin welcoming Goytisolo's position and describing him as playing the true role of writers as "voices of conscience who can exercise the freedom—and even responsibility—to stand up to unjust power." In fact, dozens of Libyan intellectuals in exile sent a message of thanks to Goytisolo in which they said:

> By publicly turning down the Gaddafi Prize for International Literature in its first year, in spite of the attractive prize money, you have struck a principled blow against the dictator Gaddafi, who thought that with the money plundered from Libyans he could buy the consciences of writers.

Those in charge of the Gaddafi prize were faced with a big problem. If they cancelled the prize it would be a big scandal, and if they offered it to another major international writer it was very possible that he would turn it down like Goytisolo, and that would be a double scandal. Although the prize was basically intended for a major international writer, the organizers overlooked this stipulation and sought out an Arab who would agree to accept the prize.

They found what they were looking for in Egyptian critic Gaber Asfour and announced that he had won the prize. Mr. Asfour, unfortunately, ignored all this context and went to Libya to receive the prize at a big ceremony in which, of course, he praised the leader of the Libyan revolution (and the King of Kings of Africa) and lauded the great freedom Libyans enjoy. Gaber Asfour did not feel the slightest embarrassment in taking a prize that a major international writer had rejected in solidarity with the Libyan people against the despotic Gaddafi regime. It seems that the amount of 150,000 euros was too much for Asfour to resist. The strange thing is that, after taking the check from Gaddafi, Asfour quickly came back to Egypt to hold spirited seminars to defend *A Thousand and One Nights*. After that, can one believe Gaber Asfour when he defends freedom of creativity?

Freedoms are inseparable and we cannot defend freedom of creativity in isolation from other general freedoms. Creative freedom, although of great importance, acquires its value only in the context of defending the rights, the freedom, and the dignity of people in general. The difference between Gaber Asfour's position and that of Goytisolo is exactly the difference between interests and principles, between wrong and right. When all our intellectuals act like Goytisolo, only then will despotism end and the future begin.

Democracy is the solution.

May 18, 2010

The Fate of Ibrahim Eissa

I n the 1980s I applied for a grant to study in the United States and
one of the conditions was to pass an examination in English as a
foreign language, the TOEFL. I took the exam in Ewart Hall at the
American University in Cairo and the room was full of young doctors and
engineers who, like me, were applying to go abroad to study. That day I
asked everyone I met if they would like to stay in the United States if they
had a chance, and the answer was a firm yes. In fact many wanted to leave
Egypt and go to any country whatsoever. At the time I thought what a
devastating loss this was for Egypt. The country desperately needed these
doctors and engineers but as soon as they finished their education, they
were emigrating to other countries.

That led me to another question: Why did these young people want to
escape Egypt? Poverty was not the reason because with a little patience
and hard work they could work in Egypt for reasonable salaries, whereas
in the West they would often have to do menial work well beneath their
qualifications. The fundamental reason they were emigrating was frustration and a sense that the situation in Egypt is unfair and topsy-turvy.
Causes mostly do not lead to the right results, hard work is never a prereq-
uisite for promotion, and competence is not the criterion for obtaining a
good job. In fact making a fortune usually has nothing to do with talent or
effort. Everything one earns in democratic countries through hard work
and merit can be obtained in Egypt through personal contacts and cun-
ning. All the things that entitle you to promotion there are not enough
to get ahead in Egypt. On the contrary, if you are talented in Egypt, you
face a major problem and would be better off if you were average or even
a dim-witted failure, first because the system is designed for average

people and suffocates those with talent, and second because your future depends first and foremost on your relationships rather than your just deserts. To have talent in Egypt is a burden because it gives rise to malice and envy, and many people will come forward to crush it. If you are talented in Egypt, you face three options: you can emigrate to a democratic country that respects talents and appreciates competence, where you can work hard day after day until you become like Ahmed Zewail, Mohamed ElBaradei, Magdi Yacoub, and their like; you can offer your talents to a despotic system, agreeing to be its servant and a tool for oppressing, abusing, and cheating Egyptians; or you can decide to preserve your honor, in which case you will meet the same fate as Ibrahim Eissa.

Eissa is one of the most gifted, honest, and courageous journalists in Egypt. With his dazzling talent and with almost no resources, he managed to make *al-Dustur* newspaper into a distinctive landmark on the Egyptian and Arab media scene, and like a great master, he has not been content with his own professional achievement but also sees it as his duty to sponsor young talent. At *al-Dustur* he introduced dozens of new names, all of whom came to him as young reporters. He gave them love, encouraged them, and taught them to fly until they soared high in the sky of the Egyptian press. If Ibrahim Eissa had appeared in a democratic country, he would now be living crowned with honors for his talent and his work. Unfortunately he is in Egypt, where the despotic regime cannot allow you to be talented and honorable at the same time. Ibrahim Eissa did not oppose the government, he opposed the system. He did not launch attacks on those responsible for the sewage system or the telephone network, he directed his critiques at the head of the regime personally. He called for real democratic change through free and fair elections and regular change at the top. He took a firm stand against any attempt to transfer power from father to son as though Egypt were a poultry farm. Ibrahim Eissa managed to turn *al-Dustur* into an important training ground for journalists and an open house for all patriots. Any Egyptian with a just grievance would find *al-Dustur* on his side and any writer who had an article banned in any other newspaper could automatically have it published in *al-Dustur*. It was a newspaper for all Egyptians, defending the truth without fear or favor.

The regime tried to silence Ibrahim Eissa in every possible way. It tried to wear him down with absurd trials and frivolous lawsuits. It intimidated him and threatened to detain him because he dared to ask questions about President Mubarak's health, then decided at the last minute to pardon him.

It tried to buy him by commissioning him to present television programs that would bring him an income, in the belief that he would take his livelihood into account and shut up, but with the passage of time it was clear that his conscience was not for sale. Ibrahim Eissa held fast to the torch of truth, always saying what he believed and always doing what he said. As popular and international pressure for democratic change mounted in Egypt, the regime faced a predicament and grew nervous. Ibrahim Eissa had become more than the regime could tolerate. At this point a masterly plan was drawn up to destroy Ibrahim Eissa, and the plan was rapidly put into effect stage by stage. There appeared on the scene a man by the name of Sayed Badawi, of whom nothing was known except that he was wealthy and owned the al-Hayat television channels, which suggests that he had the approval of senior regime officials. Badawi spent vast amounts of money to win leadership of the Wafd Party and then spent more money to persuade the party to play the role of token opposition in the farce of the next rigged elections. This was the first task Badawi accomplished for the regime. Then came his second task. Suddenly we saw Badawi buying *al-Dustur* and saying from the first that the newspaper's political line would not change and that his principle is always to keep management and editorial separate. Then another owner appeared alongside Badawi, a man by the name of Reda Edward, someone who has never had anything to do with the press. The two partners performed their task with high professionalism. Mr. Edward talked tough and flaunted his loyalty to the regime, while Badawi smiled sweetly as he gave everyone hugs and kisses and kind words. But the plan was carried out with precision.

On the very day ownership of *al-Dustur* was officially transferred, Badawi's first decision was to dismiss Ibrahim Eissa arbitrarily and contemptuously. After that everything was carefully calculated. The young journalists, shocked to see Badawi mistreat their mentor, protested and staged a sit-in. They were an easy challenge. Badawi gave them new contracts with good salaries to make them forget what happened. The union of journalists, meanwhile, found itself in a situation unprecedented in the Egyptian press. The union board took the matter seriously and demanded that Ibrahim Eissa be reinstated because he was dismissed arbitrarily and illegally. At this point union leader Makram Mohamed Ahmed, a leading admirer of President Mubarak, his wisdom, and his achievements, came into the picture. Ahmed rushed hither and thither and held lengthy meetings that concluded with him advising Ibrahim Eissa to seek redress through the legal system (some effective union leadership!). In this way the goal was accomplished and Ibrahim Eissa was dismissed as editor of *al-Dustur*, the newspaper he had created with his intellect and his effort. It is plainly obvious that Badawi and Reda Edward are merely the latest model of regime men.

The question is why were all these plots and maneuvers carried out and millions of pounds wasted in order to get rid of a talented and honorable writer whose only assets are his ideas and his pen? Why didn't the regime devote all that effort to saving millions of Egyptians from the misery they live in? *Al-Dustur* is finished, but it has gone down in Egyptian history as a great national and journalistic experiment. The regime may have succeeded in dismissing Ibrahim Eissa as editor of *al-Dustur* but it will never be able to remove him from the roll of honor where Egypt records the names of honorable and righteous Egyptians. And there is one thing that Sayed Badawi and those who drew up the plan with him did not reckon on: the Ibrahim Eissa who created *al-Dustur* can create dozens of other newspapers and the tide of change in Egypt will surely triumph because it is in defense of truth and justice, while supporters of the regime are defending injustice, oppression, and evil. Egypt has risen and no one, whoever he may be, can stand between Egypt and the future.

Democracy is the solution.

October 12, 2010